Eating God's Words

The Life of Jeremiah

Leader's Guide
by Hans Boersma

CRC PUBLICATIONS
Grand Rapids, Michigan

Scripture quotations in this publication are from the HOLY BIBLE, NEW INTERNATIONAL VERSION, © 1973, 1978, 1984, International Bible Society. Used by permission of Zondervan Bible Publishers.

Revelation Series is published by CRC Publications, 2850 Kalamazoo Ave. SE, Grand Rapids, MI 49560. 1-800-333-8300.

The Life of Jeremiah: Eating God's Words (leader's guide)

ISBN 1-56212-381-5

10 9 8 7 6 5 4 3 2 1

Contents

Study guides and additional leader's guides may be ordered by writing CRC Publications at 2850 Kalamazoo Ave. SE, Grand Rapids, MI 49560, or by calling toll-free 1-800-333-8300. Please refer to the following product numbers as needed: Leader's Guide, #1312-0240R; Study Guide, #1312-0200R; Large-Print Study Guide, #1312-0205R.

Introduction

This *Revelation Series* leader's guide provides background information and discussion suggestions for the thirteen lessons of *The Life of Jeremiah: Eating God's Words*, an in-depth Bible study for adults. Dr. Hans Boersma, who has served as a pastor in the Canadian Reformed Churches and as a Christian school teacher, wrote this leader's guide and the accompanying study guide. Each member of your group should have a study guide to use during this Bible study.

Using This Leader's Guide

This leader's guide is intended to be only what its title conveys: a guide. It is not meant to be followed like a cookbook, step by step. It offers suggestions rather than prescriptions. As a discussion leader, you should adapt all materials and procedures in this leader's guide to suit the needs and abilities of your group members.

For each lesson in the accompanying study guide, this leader's guide adds background and supplementary material that you, as leader, can share as you see fit to enhance your group's discussion of the lesson. This guide also includes answers to the General Discussion questions posed in the study guide. These answers are meant to provide you with a beginning point for discussion, if you find that useful. No claim is made for completeness, however, or for having the "last word."

A feature that we've recently added to the *Revelation Series* is Ideas for Small Groups. You'll notice a brief lesson plan for small group use in both the study guide and the leader's guide, with a few additional tips included in the plan found in the leader's guide. If you're the leader of a small group, we hope you find this feature useful as you and your group explore this in-depth Bible study together. (See below for more information on Small Group Study.)

Use what you can in this leader's guide, but please feel free to adapt, substitute, and revise. Pose your own questions and seek answers based on your study and on the insights of group members. Your ultimate goal is not simply to cover the lesson but to lead the group into an encounter with the living Word of God.

Using the Study Guide

Each person in your group should have a study guide to use at home and during your meetings. The material for each lesson in the study guide includes the Scripture passage to be studied, thought-provoking notes and commentary on the Scripture, and several discussion questions that will help your group apply the Scripture to their lives today.

Some groups like to read the Scripture passage and the lesson notes during their meeting—and that can be very useful for making the material fresh in everyone's mind while doing the lesson together. Because of the volume of material in each lesson, however, we suggest that group members spend twenty minutes or so familiarizing themselves with the lesson material at home ahead of time so that when everyone meets together any reading will serve as review and the group can move efficiently into discussion time.

Note: You'll notice that the Ideas for Small Groups (discussed in the Small Group Study section below) include some suggestions for reading and discussion as well as a few notes about opening and closing in prayer and doing various group projects. As leader, feel free to use and adapt any of this information as you wish, even if you happen not to prefer the small group approach. Various kinds of study groups are bound to find many of the lesson suggestions useful.

Your Role as Leader

You are more the leader of a study group than the teacher of a class. The essential difference, we suggest, is that a leader/group situation is less structured and formal than a teacher/class situation. The teacher is somewhat of an "authority" on his or her subject; the leader is less so. The teacher may be somewhat separated from the class; the leader is part of the group. The teacher carefully works toward specific objectives, often centered on mastery of content; the leader works more with process and people than with objectives, seeking to encourage each person to participate and grow.

Aren't teachers also leaders, and leaders also teachers? Of course, but we draw this leader/teacher distinction to help you visualize your role within the study group, the role toward which this leader's guide is slanted. Together leader and group seek to understand and obey the Word of God. Together they share their questions and insights. Together they pray for one another and strengthen one another.

Small Group Study

Each of the following lessons contains a basic lesson plan that's designed to adapt this in-depth Bible study to small group use. You'll find the lesson plan under Ideas for Small Groups at the end of each lesson's material in both the study guide and this leader's guide.

Small groups tend to use various kinds of formats in their meetings. Some small groups meet for a couple of hours every week; others meet for an hour every two or three weeks. Some study the Bible for an hour and then divide into groups of two or three for an additional hour of confidential prayer-and-share time; others study the Bible for a half to three-quarters of an hour and then spend about fifteen minutes in sharing and prayer. The formats may vary from one small group strategy to the next, but each one will usually include most of the elements found in the basic plan suggested here. So whatever the format you're used to, we hope you'll find most of the elements in the lesson plan adaptable to your group and its particular needs. Feel free to add, omit, reorganize, or change any of the elements you find in this basic plan.

The lesson plan includes the essential elements of a small group study, so if you're new to the small group approach and you'd like to try it, this will give you a taste of what small group study is like. Many groups that have tried the small group approach find it extremely rewarding, mainly because the elements of sharing one's feelings and giving one's personal input can become trust-building and friendship-building and confidence-building when coupled with group confidentiality and integrity. Within the body of Christ and with direction provided by the Word of God, this small group activity results in fellowship and spiritual growth, to God's glory. While being inwardly focused in the areas of sharing and developing personal expression, the small group approach, if it's healthy, also focuses on looking and reaching outward for the benefit of others. Both of these inward and outward focuses are essential in the church and in the individual Christian life.

Here's a brief overview of the basic plan you'll find under Ideas for Small Groups in each lesson:

- The lesson plan is divided into several timed sections to help you keep pace for your group's meeting time. The suggested times for each section total about 60-75 minutes. Some groups will use 75 minutes or more; others will use 60 or even a little less. Use whatever time your group needs or is most comfortable with. Never feel pressured to work through all of the discussion questions if you don't have enough time. Pick and choose the ones you and your group think are appropriate or most applicable.
- For the Opening of your session we suggest a brief time for beginning with prayer and with sharing your past week's experiences, especially with regard to any personal and spiritual goals you've set. Then we invite you to reflect on a focus question to keep in mind as you move into Bible study.
- The Growing section of your session includes some brief suggestions on reading the Scripture passage and the study-guide notes, if your group likes to read before getting into discussion. Then follow suggestions for using some of the General Discussion questions along with process questions that are designed specifically for small group use. These questions generally guide your thinking process from *what you think* to *how you can help others* in relation to the topic you're studying in a lesson.
- The next section is Goalsetting, in which you commit to a personal spiritual goal as a result of the Bible study you have just completed.
- The Closing section of your session includes a time for sharing prayer concerns and praises before you join with the group in a concluding prayer.
- Several sessions also include Group Project ideas that some or all of your group can try. The projects are for study or hands-on work or both, and their purpose is for outreach or for teaching that can enhance the group's outward focus.

Tips for Good Discussion

Lively discussion is vital to any adult Bible-study group. It's the rare leader who really wants to do all the talking and the rare group member who's willing to sit and listen without ever expressing his or her views. Only a good deal of practice will help you become a truly effective discussion leader, but you should know a few general principles for good discussion. Here's our list:

- Create a comfortable, informal setting for learning. Have participants seated in a circle rather than in rows. As leader, sit with your group members, not in front of them.
- Ask questions of the entire group before asking individuals to respond.
- Allow plenty of time for responses to questions. Don't be afraid of silence—people need time to reflect and think. When you ask a particularly difficult question, request three to five minutes of silence, giving members time to think. This approach delays those who always answer quickly and sometimes superficially; it gives the slow and deep thinkers a chance to participate.
- Avoid any needless repetition of group members' answers.
- If necessary, direct group members' responses to those of others in the group: "Pete, do you agree with Joan on this point?" Avoid giving people the sense that they are answering questions for you, the leader.
- Be appreciative of all responses. Almost every answer includes something worth noting (approval can be communicated nonverbally with a smile or nod). Often "wrong answers" are a result of a misunderstood question. Be sure of yourself before you directly disagree with any response.
- Occasionally assign a question or task to small groups rather than to the entire group. Although it may take more time to complete the exercise, smaller groups encourage participation from all members. In order to make small group exercises effective, clearly define each group's task or question and set a definite time limit for their work. Their reports to the entire group are beneficial but optional.
- If a question is intended for general discussion, it may have more than one answer or solution. Be open. Don't try to press your own solution on the group.
- Be ready to discuss questions that group members may raise in addition to the questions found in your Bible-study material.
- Limit your group's discussions. There's no point in prolonging a good thing until it drops. If the discussion goes off on an unprofitable tangent, say something like "That's interesting, and maybe we can discuss it later, but let's get back to the issue. . . ." As leader, you'll want to keep the discussion relevant to the question.
- Summarize long discussions. Sometimes the main point of a discussion can become lost in details. Then either you—or perhaps a group member—should summarize what the group has said.
- Adapt all material and procedures in this leader's guide to suit the needs and abilities of your group members, your own skills and interests, and the amount of time you have.
- Periodically ask the group how you're doing. Are there any procedural changes they would like to suggest?

The Adult as Student

The adults in your group are in many ways ideal students. For one thing, they're there because they *want* to be. No one tells them, "Go to Bible study today, or I'll report you to the elders." Unlike children and young people, adults are volunteer students, just as you are a volunteer leader. That means they're motivated, as eager to learn as you are to lead.

And they want to learn something of value, something substantial. They'll look to you to help them discover new information, new Bible-reading skills, new insights and applications. Therefore, being well prepared is highly recommended for any leader who wants to do well in the adult study group. Be careful, though, not to come armed with so much "substance" that you need to lecture to get it across. (Some adult groups are passive enough to let you get away with this!) It's better to come with a well-prepared lesson that will involve you *and* your group members in learning *together* from God's Word. Learn to talk to your group, asking, "What can *we* learn from this passage?" rather than demanding, "Tell *me* how this verse might affect *your* daily walk." And, of course, admit your own ignorance when you don't know something; "I don't know" is an honest answer that adults will respect.

Don't assume your group members know everything either. Some may be relatively new Christians, unfamiliar with much of the Bible. Others may be enrolled in their first adult-education class and, having been out of the classroom or study setting for many years, may be as nervous as a teenager on the first day of school: "What if

I say something stupid—or, worse yet, heretical?" Patience and empathy are qualities that leaders should pray for.

Remember that adults come to this study with a great deal of experience—if not in theology, at least in the art of living. That means, among other things, that they want their learning to be practical, applicable to their daily routines. They want to learn not only what David had in mind when he penned his guilt in Psalm 51 but also how his guilt expresses *theirs,* how his prayer for forgiveness can shape their own. Try for a balance between explanation and application, abstract and specific, theory and practice. Respect and draw on the vast amount of wisdom and experience adults bring.

Your group will expect a lot from you as their leader and guide. But sometimes it's hard to know just how much to expect from them. Leaders who look first for large numbers and consistent attendance may be disappointed. Don't take the lack of either as a personal failure. Keep in mind that adults are busy and often face demanding schedules. There are sick kids to stay home for, dinners to be prepared, visits to Grandma and Grandpa, and many other reasons for missing a session here and there. Better to be thankful for the few who do show up than to complain about the ones who are not there. Build on what God has provided, trusting in the Spirit to equip you and your group to learn together from his Word.

Being a leader of adults can be a serious, humbling business. While you're preparing for a lesson, the doubts come thick and fast: "How did *I* get talked into this? I'm no Bible scholar . . . no teacher. . . . How do I dare instruct my friends from church in the Word of God?" Then be reminded that leading a group is more than methodology, more than a grab bag of skills. It's a calling for which God's Spirit will equip you. And when you meet with your group, Christ will be there by your side, through his Word and Spirit, gathering his people. This is what makes your role possible . . . and profitable.

Our prayers go with you as you lead others.

The Education, Worship, and Evangelism
Department of CRC Publications

Evaluations

When you finish this Bible study, please invite group members to fill out the evaluation form at the back of the study guide and mail it to us at the address below. Any suggestions will be helpful to us in developing other studies in the *Revelation Series.* Thank you!

Please mail evaluations to

Revelation Series / The Life of Jeremiah
CRC Publications
2850 Kalamazoo Ave. SE
Grand Rapids, MI 49560

1 Jeremiah's Call

Jeremiah 1

A Source of Inspiration

For centuries Jeremiah's call has been a source of inspiration to believers. Already in the days of the early church the apostle Paul looked back on the event. He understood his own calling in line with the prophetic tradition, noting that God "set [him] apart from birth" (Gal. 1:15; see Isa. 49:1; Jer. 1:5). The first chapter of Jeremiah has often been used to encourage God's people in responding to the Lord's call. This chapter has provided much-needed strength for those who have heard the call to serve officially or in other capacities in the church. And there is good reason for this practice. The chapter pits God's provision over against human fear and inability. At the same time, in the concrete experience of one man's struggle with his call, this chapter calls on people of all times to place God's word at the center of their lives. In this chapter we see how God chooses and appoints Jeremiah to bring his all-encompassing word—especially a message of judgment—to his people and to the world.

God's Choice of Jeremiah

Before coming to Jeremiah with a job description, the Lord makes this young man aware of the significance of his call and, in so doing, encourages him. Jeremiah's call, as described at the beginning of his book of prophecy, carries much significance. The Lord says he "knew" Jeremiah before forming him in the womb (1:5). In the Scriptures, knowledge reaches far beyond the possession of mere factual information; it refers to an intimate familiarity and a close relationship (see Ps. 139:1-6, 13-16, 23-24; see also Gen. 4:1, RSV). Before he had formed Jeremiah in the womb, the Lord had already planned whom he was going to use as his prophet. He already had a deep insight into who this prophet was going to be and what his character would be like. God set Jeremiah apart prior to his birth, consecrating him to his prophetic task. Since this appointment goes back before his birth and his being formed in the womb, Jeremiah knows from the outset that the Lord himself stands behind his call and his ministry. This knowledge is something Jeremiah may draw deeply upon in the difficult times that will surely come.

A Time of Upheaval

Jeremiah's call came at a time of upheaval, both nationally and internationally, both religiously and politically. The Assyrian empire in the east had been the dominant world power for several centuries. By 722 B.C. the ten northern tribes of Israel had fallen completely into Assyria's hands, and many thousands of them were deported to Assyria. The Assyrian dominance, however, was not to stay. In the year 627 the Assyrian king Ashurbanipal died. His death was symbolic for the decline of his empire, which began to deteriorate around the same time. Before long the thriving Babylonian empire led by Nabopolasser—with his son, Nebuchadnezzar, as army commander—replaced the control of the Assyrians.

Josiah, the young king of Judah, took the opportunity to assert his independence from Assyria as well as from its gods. He started a sweeping reform a few years before Ashurbanipal died (2 Chron. 34:3-7). The worship of the Lord had been a shambles throughout the long reign of Josiah's grandfather, Manasseh (697-42), as well as during the two-year reign of Josiah's father, Amon (642-40). Now it was Josiah's turn. His reforms climaxed in the recovery of the book of the law in 622 B.C. (2 Kings 22-23; 2 Chron. 34:8, 14).

In the thirteenth year of Josiah's reign the Lord called Jeremiah (Jer. 1:2). Both men were young: Josiah must have been about twenty-one years old, while estimates of Jeremiah's age vary. Jeremiah uses his young age as an excuse to decline God's call (1:6). He probably was not much younger or older than the pious king who had begun initiating reforms about five years earlier. The book of Jeremiah does not discuss the relationship between these two men. Although Josiah's reforms must have brought Jeremiah great joy, they appear not to have touched the soul of the nation. This explains how Jeremiah could be called to denounce the idolatry and complacency that persisted in Judah at a time when Josiah had begun to implement worship reforms in Jerusalem.

Universal Significance

Once we have a sense of this backdrop to Jeremiah's call, the Lord's first words to Jeremiah—about God's knowledge and consecration of this prophet (1:5)—take on new meaning. Jeremiah needed to know that God was the one standing behind his call. The word of the Lord is central in this episode from beginning to end. The passage starts off with the sentence "The *word* of the LORD came to me" (1:4), and it ends with the phrase "*declares* the LORD" (1:19). One can only speak God's word after having heard it. Our speaking can only be a response to God's acting or speaking. Accordingly the Lord touches Jeremiah's mouth as a symbol that he will put his words in the prophet's mouth (1:9).

There is nothing the word of God does not cover. No moment of time, no aspect of life escapes the auspices of God's word. This word is the same word the Lord told Moses to speak. In fact, the story of Jeremiah's call portrays him in some ways as another Moses. Jeremiah's objection in 1:6 is similar to the one Moses had at the burning bush (Ex. 4:10). Just as Moses was once told to speak everything the Lord commanded him (Ex. 7:2), so Jeremiah is told the same thing (Jer. 1:7, 17). God had told Moses that one day there would be a prophet who would be like him: "I will raise up for them a prophet like you from among their brothers; I will put my words in his mouth, and he will tell them everything I command him" (Deut. 18:18). In Jeremiah God provides such a prophet. The most comforting thing for Jeremiah is that the Lord adds, "Do not be afraid of them, for I am with you and will rescue you" (1:8; see 1:19). Amid all the opposition Jeremiah will face, the Lord promises to "rescue" him, just as he promised to "rescue" Moses and Israel from Egypt (Ex. 3:8). Jeremiah will face a daunting forty years (626-587 B.C.), just as Moses faced. But standing in this Mosaic tradition, Jeremiah is allowed to know that he has a God-ordained place in the history of God's salvation. God ensures that his prophetic word is spoken throughout history.

The universal significance of God's word also emerges when the Lord says he has appointed Jeremiah "as a prophet to the nations" (1:5). Jeremiah is appointed "over nations and kingdoms" (1:10). To be sure, apart from the prophetic announcements in Jeremiah 46-51 (often called the "oracles against the nations"), most of Jeremiah's prophecies concern Judah itself. But in 1:10 there is no contrast between Judah and other "nations and kingdoms." In chapter 18 the Lord tells Jeremiah to go to the local potter's house. That well-known story uses some of the same words we find in chapter 1 (see 18:7-10). There we find the language of uprooting, tearing down, and destroying, of building up and planting applied to "nations and kingdoms" (1:10). In the story of the potter's house that same language is applied to Judah (18:11). In other words, Judah is simply one of the "nations and kingdoms" and cannot boast of her status with God. The Lord makes clear here that membership among his people does not guarantee salvation. The Lord shows no partiality. Judah is one among many recipients of God's all-encompassing, prophetic word.

Two Visions

The Lord's word to Judah is primarily one of judgment. The verbs "to uproot" and "to plant" present us with agricultural images, while the other four verbs in 1:10 place us in the world of demolition and construction. The words Jeremiah has to speak will be powerful—first of all in announcing God's judgment, but then also in looking beyond the judgment to restoration. (For further reading, see J. G. McConville's book on Jeremiah, which bears the characteristic title *Judgment and Promise* [Leicester: Apollos; Winona Lake, Ind.: Eisenbrauns, 1993]). Already in the call of Jeremiah, the Lord shows a glimpse of the end-time reality of a new covenant, when his blessing in Christ will finally and definitively snuff out his curse.

The Lord only briefly mentions here his promise of building and planting. Many prophecies of judgment, much personal abuse toward Jeremiah, and the great curse of the exile will precede that final restoration. The prophecies of judgment will come first. And there is no doubt about their fulfillment. Jeremiah's vision of an almond-tree branch makes clear that his prophecies will come true (1:11-12). The Lord is awake and watching (*shoqed*) over that fulfillment just as certainly as the almond tree (*shaqed*) is a "waking tree" that wakes up and blossoms before any other tree.

The predominance of judgment comes to the fore in the next vision Jeremiah receives: a boiling cauldron "tilting away from the north" toward Judah (1:13). This image of disaster is Jeremiah's first warning against Judah, which forty years later will result in the destruction of Jerusalem and Judah's exile to Babylon (587 B.C.). The Lord himself provides some words of explanation with the picture of the boiling pot: "Kings will come and set up their thrones in the entrance of the gates of Jerusalem" (1:15). Jeremiah describes the fulfillment of this vision in more detail in his account of the fall of the city in chapter 39. There we find the Babylonian officials taking their seats in the "Middle Gate" of Jerusalem (39:3).

This fall of the city will not simply be the Babylonians' doing; it will also be the fulfillment of Jeremiah's prophecies, of God's word to Judah. God himself will summon the enemies. Their conquest of the land of Israel will be God's judgment on the people for their idolatry, their abandonment of the Mosaic covenant. The curse of Deuteronomy, predicted and warned against by Moses (Deut. 28:15-68; 31:14-29), will be fulfilled after a last warning call from Jeremiah. So Jeremiah can be certain that his role is a crucial one in God's program.

As their conversation draws to a close, the Lord encourages Jeremiah one last time not to be afraid. And, as we note in the study guide, it is not his enemies but the Lord who should really instill fear in him (Jer. 1:17). The Lord uses three different images to strengthen his prophet. In God's strength Jeremiah will be "a fortified city, an iron pillar and a bronze wall" (1:18). The God of the exodus will rescue his prophet from his enemies (1:19). Even though Jeremiah's life may not seem to reflect this invincibility, we find that (1) the prophet's faithfulness to God is itself a form of rescue, and (2) in restoring his people after the exile in a new covenant, God rescued also his Servant (Jesus—see Isa. 52:13-53:12) and his message. This rescue is ultimately realized in a renewed Israel in Christ, a new people of God including believers from all nations.

Additional Notes

1:10—The verbs used in this verse recur throughout the book of Jeremiah to express the twin theme of judgment and restoration (see 2:21; 12:14-17; 18:7-10; 24:6; 31:4-5, 28, 40; 32:41; 33:7; 42:10; 45:4; see also the section The Blessing and Curse of the Covenant in lesson 8 of this leader's guide).

1:18—At a later date, when Jeremiah is despondent about the opposition he receives, the Lord encourages him by reminding him of these words of his original call. Jeremiah will again be a "fortified wall of bronze" (15:20; see lesson 7).

General Discussion

1. *As you begin this Bible study, spend a few minutes talking together about why you've chosen to study the life of Jeremiah. What expectations do you have about doing this study? If you like, share a few details that you may already know about this prophet and his place in God's redemption plan. Or share any curiosities you may have.*

This question may help you and the rest of your group gain a sense of where everyone is coming from as you begin this Bible study together. Invite candid responses from everyone in the group, and use this exercise as a means to cover background material mentioned in the above leader's notes, as it applies to your group.

2. *Many people live in fear and seem unable to shed their worries and anxieties. Where do our worries and anxieties come from? What insights can we gain from Jeremiah's call that can help us respond to fears in ourselves and encourage others in dealing with their fears?*

This question is intended to lead directly into the heart of this lesson's Scripture passage and how it has a message for us today. External and internal factors combine to cause reactions of fear. All sorts of situations, many of them beyond our control, may create uncertainty—or perhaps even bring predictable troubles. And whether our uncertainty results in fear and anxiety depends not only on external factors but also on internal ones. Fear naturally results when our faith, or trust, in something gives way. Look at the apostle Peter. He had amazing faith when he stepped out of a boat on a storm-tossed sea and began walking toward Jesus. But when he looked around at the crashing waves and heard the howling wind, he doubted, his faith withered and gave way to fear, and he began sinking like a rock (see Matt. 14:22-33). We don't know if he ever walked on water again, but we do know that a while later he had enough faith, by the Holy Spirit, to stand up to the religious leaders who had killed Jesus and to say, "We must obey God rather than men!" (Acts 5:29). By the Spirit of God we can have enough faith to stand up against God's enemies, even if we might be killed for doing so.

Jeremiah was called by God at a time of great political/military and religious uncertainty, and his message from the Lord was sure to result in sharp confrontation with the mindset of his day. Jeremiah had God's promise, however, that he would be "a fortified city, an iron pillar, and a bronze wall" to stand up against all the officials and people of the land of Judah (Jer. 1:18). How do we respond to the various situations in which God calls for our faithful response? This passage gives us much reason for a bold and courageous response: we stand in a tradition of faithful prophets that includes Moses, Jeremiah, and, above all, Jesus. In and through him God has promised to rescue us, "to enable us to serve him without fear" (Luke 1:74). It may be a helpful exercise for you and your group to list various ways in which the Lord provides encouragement to Jeremiah in the passage we are studying for this lesson (see 1:8, 10, 11-12, 18-19 for examples).

3. *In reaction to Jeremiah's call, someone might say, "Jeremiah received a clear, unmistakable call from God. We often wish we were in that position. If only we knew what the Lord's will was, we'd be sure to follow it." In light of the Scripture for this lesson, how would you deal with this comment?*

One way to respond to this statement is to note that in many ways we do know God's will for our lives, through the study and preaching of his Word. Since the outpouring of the Holy Spirit on Pentecost we have had the Spirit of God in our hearts convicting us of what is sinful and what is righteous and guiding us "into all truth" as we seek to apply God's Word in our lives (John 16:8-13).

Another response may be to point out a mistake people sometimes make when they think they have to follow a plan God has for their lives. God does not usually let us know what his plan is for our lives. Even Jeremiah was told only that he would be a prophet of God, that he would prophesy judgment and restoration, that he would receive opposition in doing so, and that God would nonetheless rescue him. Is there anything here that does not apply to the greatest Prophet, Jesus (see Isa. 50:4-9; Luke 22:63-24:8; Phil. 2:5-11), and through him also to all who belong to him (Luke 21:12-19; Rom. 8:33-39; 2 Cor. 1:5)?

As they live out the pattern of hardship, of strength from the Spirit during times of opposition, and of subsequent glory in Christ, Christians search not so much for God's plan but for his will in their everyday lives. Bruce Waltke in his book *Finding the Will of God: A Pagan Notion?* (Gresham, Ore.: Vision House, 1995) provides six helpful guidelines for doing this: (1) read your Bible; (2) develop a heart for God; (3) seek wise counsel; (4) look for God's providence; (5) ask, "Does this make sense?"; and (6) be aware that sometimes God may directly intervene in our lives to give direction.

Invite group members also to ponder the danger of using the statement in question 3 as an excuse not to follow God's will when deep down we really know what he wants from us.

4. *What does this passage teach you about the character of God?*

The Lord reveals himself in various wonderful ways in this chapter. Group members will probably come up with answers like these:

- We learn of the priority of God's grace: God's knowledge and consecration of Jeremiah (1:5) precede any prophetic activity by Jeremiah.
- God takes our fears and hesitations seriously. He does not ignore Jeremiah's anxious excuse (1:6) but proceeds to encourage him.
- God wants to be served alone. God appoints Jeremiah as his prophet and eventually exiles Israel because the nation is unfaithful (1:16).
- God is faithful. He will provide as he has promised (1:12).
- God is powerful and gives strength. His call to Jeremiah came with the promise to enable him to stand firm against his enemies (1:18-19).
- Even though God's judgment may come first and may be severe, his grace, which follows, shows that God is ultimately a God who "rescues" and restores, a God of mercy (1:8, 10, 19).

Ideas for Small Groups

Opening (5-10 minutes)

Pray/Worship—As you begin your study on the life of Jeremiah, give thanks to the Lord for the opportunity to come together to study his Word. Give praise that because you belong to the New Testament people of God you may find your identity in Jesus, the great Prophet, who brought the old covenant to a close and placed us in the new. Ask the Lord for open hearts and minds so that you may grasp what he has to say to you today through the call of

Jeremiah. Pray also that the Spirit will fill you with strength to fulfill God's will in your lives.

You may wish to add a worship element at this point or at the end of your session by singing a familiar song about being open to God's call in our lives—for example, "Take My Life and Let It Be" or "Here I Am, Lord." (As leader, be sure to provide songbooks, if necessary.)

Share—Introduce yourselves to each other if you haven't met before. If you are beginning a new study season, and you know each other already, use this opportunity to briefly share together what you hope this study of Jeremiah will mean to you individually, to your study group, to your church, and to the broader community. (This exercise overlaps somwhat with General Discussion question 1.)

Focus—Throughout this lesson try to keep yourself (and the discussion) focused on the question *How is God encouraging me to follow his will?*

Growing (35-50 minutes)

Read (Optional)

Before going into your discussion time, you may wish to read Jeremiah 1 together. If you like, you could make this a responsive reading between two persons or two groups, with one person or group reading Jeremiah's part (including the narration) and the other reading the Lord's part.

Discuss

For your discussion time, you'll need to use General Discussion question 2 as a springboard into the main message of Jeremiah 1 for us today. Questions 1, 3, and 4 may also be helpful, depending on the needs and interests of your group. The following process questions pick up on the theme raised by question 2.

On dealing with my fears and weaknesses:

- Do you have any fears, weaknesses, or excuses in relation to your service to God? Share them with the group, if you feel comfortable doing so. What has Jeremiah's call taught you about dealing with the fears you might have?
- Mention one or two areas in your life in which God calls on you to hesitate no longer but to place your trust in his faithfulness.
- How can (or do) you as a congregation build each other up and spur one another on to obedience in the Lord? (See Hebrews 10:23-25; then look up Ephesians 4:1-16; 5:19-21.)
- Jeremiah had to bring the twin message of judgment (first) and grace (second). Now that Christ has come and has given us a new covenant, we can bring the good news of God's salvation. How do you bring this message? With whom do you share it?

Goalsetting (5 minutes)

Try to work on the following goal in the coming week:

- With Jeremiah I want to place my fears and anxieties in the Lord's hand and to follow his call. I trust that God's Spirit will give me the strength to do that in the following way:

Closing (5-10 minutes)

Preparing for Prayer

At this point invite group members to mention some things they would like the others in the group to remember in prayer. Of course, no one should feel forced to mention something. Also remember in prayer the focus of this lesson and the goals that group members may have set.

Prayer

With Jeremiah, address God as "Sovereign Lord," admitting that sometimes we all have fears, worries, inadequacies, and a lack of trust. Ask God that everyone in the group may have complete trust in him. Bring before God the various prayer requests mentioned by the group members, or invite them to join in and pray for each other. Also thank God for the message and the example he has given us in the prophet Jeremiah—and especially in Jesus, our great Prophet and Savior.

2 The Two Bad Sisters

Jeremiah 3:1-18

After the description of Jeremiah's call in chapter 1, we turn to the next section of the book (2:1-4:4), which introduces the problems that will be dealt with throughout Jeremiah's forty years as a prophet: Judah's backsliding, her apostasy from God, and her need to repent and turn to the Lord. Several of the themes that play a role in these chapters are worked out in the remainder of the book: God's call to Israel and Judah to turn around, the prospect of exile, and the assurance of a renewed relationship between God and his people.

Israel and Judah

Already in chapter 2 the relationship between Israel and Judah comes to the fore. Israel (the ten tribes in the north) and Judah (the two tribes in the south—Judah and Benjamin) have been two separate nations since the death of King Solomon (1 Kings 12). The name "Israel" in this chapter could refer either to the entire people of God, north and south combined, or to the northern kingdom as an independent entity. As the Lord reminisces about the early days of his marriage with his people, he speaks of Israel as the one, united nation that he lovingly led through the desert (2:1-3). The Lord then charges his people with unfaithfulness to the marriage covenant he has made with them. They have exchanged their God for worthless idols, thus defiling the land (2:7).

In these opening verses of chapter 2 it appears that "Israel" could refer to the one, united people of Israel. The form of the message is to the nation as a whole. As a prophet, however, Jeremiah does not really prophesy to the northern tribes. He is located in Judah, so he most likely is addressing Judah while using the form of an address to all Israel, the "house of Jacob" (2:4).

Before long within this same chapter, though, we notice a shift in the meaning of the word "Israel." Under the name of Israel the northern tribes are presented as an example to warn Judah. Israel has been conquered and deported by Assyria (722 B.C.), which should be a warning for Judah (2:14-15, 18, 36). The Lord points out that if Judah places her trust in Assyria or Egypt she will face the same fate as Israel, whose trust in Assyria led to her downfall at the hand of that very empire.

In 3:1-5 the Lord puts Judah on notice. Because of her idolatry she has made it impossible to be reconciled to the groom of her youth. As noted in the study guide, the law of Deuteronomy states that one is not allowed to take back one's wife after she has been divorced and then married to someone else (Deut. 24:1-4). The pronouncement in 3:1 reminds Judah of this law. And again the Lord charges her with defiling the land with her "prostitution and wickedness" (Jer. 3:2; see 2:7).

Next comes the story of the two bad sisters. The previous chapter prepared Jeremiah's listeners for this when it warned Judah not to follow in Israel's footsteps. Jeremiah 3:1 also provides a lead-in, with its reminder of the law's prohibition of remarriage. Translated literally, Jeremiah's names for the two sisters are "Turn-Around" and "Treacherous," as noted in the study guide. Let's take a look now at Jeremiah's play with the word "turn" in this passage.

A Call to Turn

Jeremiah's designation of Israel as "Madam Turn-Around" hooks into the central message of this passage and of the entire book. The context of this story repeatedly uses various forms of the verb "to turn" (*shuv*). A husband cannot "return" (*shuv*) to his wife after she has left him and has married another man (3:1; Deut. 24:1-4). In Jeremiah 3:12 and 3:14 the Lord twice calls on Israel to "return" (*shuv*). The Lord reflects on a time when he thought Israel would repent: "I thought you would call me 'Father' and not turn away [*shuv*] from following me" (Jer. 3:19). The Lord still calls on his apostate people Israel to come back to him: "Return [*shuv*], faithless [*shuv*] people; I will cure you of backsliding [*shuv*]" (3:22). He adds, "If you will return [*shuv*], O Israel, return [*shuv*] to me" (4:1). The entire passage of 3:1-4:4 is characterized by the verb "to turn." Invariably the use of this verb presents an appeal to Israel or Judah to turn from their idols to the husband of their youth.

The same use of the verb "to turn" is reflected in the story of the two bad sisters. First, the very name of Madam Turn-Around presents a call on Israel to turn back. Since the story is actually an appeal to Judah to look at her sister, Israel, as a warning example, the use of Israel's name is also a call on Judah to repent. The Lord says he thought Israel would "return" (*shuv*) after all her idolatry (3:7). But she did not. Judah, who had seen her sister's example, "did not return" (*shuv*) to the Lord either (3:10). In fact, Madam Turn-Around (Israel) compares favorably to Madam Treacherous (Judah). "Faithless Israel is more righteous than unfaithful Judah" (3:11). Despite the warning example of her sister's destruction, Madam Treacherous went ahead and prostituted herself anyway.

Madam Turn-Around's adultery (her idolatry) and the subsequent divorce (her exile to Assyria) formed a warning example to Madam Treacherous. This reveals something about God's dealings with the world. God's love for the world is his motivation for sending his Son (John 3:16). God's love is revealed in his death for sinners rather than for righteous people (Rom. 5:8). God's love in his Son is also the primary motivation for the church's mission to the world. This free offer of God's love does not, however, result in a free ride without commitment. Once God establishes a relationship of love with his people, he wants unwavering loyalty. Jesus said to the covenant nation of his day that it would be "more bearable for Sodom on the day of judgment" than for the cities that had witnessed most of his miracles and yet had rejected him (Matt. 11:24). The Lord's divorce (exile) of Israel should have been enough of an example to persuade Judah to turn around. But it was not to be. The question today is whether we will listen to God's wake-up call: the punishment of our sin in Christ's death on the cross.

God's call to repentance in Christ is a very practical, down-to-earth call. Our actions have to match our confession; we have to live for the Lord with all our heart (Jer. 3:10; James 2:26). And by God's grace and power we can do that (Eph. 2:8-10). Jeremiah came with the story of the two bad sisters during the reign of King Josiah (640-609 B.C.), who had initiated a major reform and had called the people of Judah back to the service of the Lord (2 Kings 22-23). Jeremiah, however, insisted that addressing God as "Father" (Jer. 3:4) and talking piously about the ark of the covenant (3:16) meant nothing as long as it was only a veneer covering hearts that remained uncircumcised and actions that were evil (4:4). Jesus' words to the covenant people of his day come to mind: "Not everyone who says to me, 'Lord, Lord,' will enter the kingdom of heaven, but only he who does the will of my Father who is in heaven" (Matt. 7:21).

The Prospect of Remarriage

By prostituting herself, Israel had left the Lord no option but to give her a "certificate of divorce" (3:8). Deuteronomy 24 stipulated that this excluded any future reconciliation. The message for Israel's sister, Judah, is obvious: if she continues her prostitution, she will also get a certificate of divorce. In other words, she will also be destroyed by her enemies, and this will mean an irreversible end to God's covenant of love with Judah. The story of the two bad sisters contains a serious warning for Judah to turn around before it is too late.

One of the remarkable features of Jeremiah, however, is that despite the overall negative character of his preaching he allows us to look beyond the threat of judgment. The law against remarriage (Deut. 24:1-4), which Jeremiah recalls in 3:1, is apparently not an absolute. Judah's sister has already been divorced. She is already in exile. According to the law, the relationship should be finished. Nonetheless, the Lord still calls even Israel back to himself. He still calls on her, along with Judah, to turn around (3:12-4:4). In fact, he looks forward to a reunion of the divided kingdom of Israel and Judah (3:18).

This renewed call on the northern kingdom does not mean Jeremiah actually preached to the Israelites who still lived in the north. Rather, the fact that the Lord still calls Israel—even after her exile to Assyria—contains a message for Judah. Judah may know that there is still hope. Not only is there hope now, if she will take the story of the two bad sisters to heart, but there will even be hope if she refuses to listen and, like her sister, be led into exile. God's love for his people will ultimately cause him to overcome the limitations of his own law against remarriage. The blessing of the covenant will outdo the curse of the covenant.

Jeremiah 3 pictures the restoration and repentance of Israel (3:14-18, 22-24). It's a picture with a question mark. Jeremiah does not explain how the restoration of Israel and Judah is possible in light of the restriction of Deuteronomy 24. But the New Testament changes the question mark into an exclamation mark in the revelation of Jesus. In a real sense he was divorced from God on the cross, taking the punishment of his people's unfaithfulness upon himself. In this way Jesus brought about both the end of the exile and the beginning of a new covenant. The Lord overcame the restriction of Deuteronomy 24 in the cross of Christ. Through him, people may once again turn to God—not in pretense but with all their hearts (Jer. 3:10), with hearts turned around by the Spirit of God (John 16:8).

Additional Notes

3:6—Jeremiah describes Israel's apostasy in terms of involvement in the fertility cults of the surrounding Canaanite nations. Israel has "gone up on every high hill and under every spreading tree and has committed adultery there." This description is similar to Hosea's earlier denouncement of the northern kingdom before the Assyrian destruction of Samaria in 722 B.C. (see Hos. 4:12-13). Jeremiah was clearly familiar with the themes of Hosea. His indebtedness to Hosea comes out at various points in the book.

3:6-7—For similar personifications of Israel and Judah in similar contexts of idolatry, see Ezekiel 16 and 23.

3:7—In his goodness the Lord allowed Judah to see Israel's idolatry and her punishment. This made Judah more responsible for her own apostasy. The New Testament similarly indicates that those who have received more grace carry a greater responsibility: Luke 12:48; 19:26; Rom. 1:18-23; 2:12-16; Heb. 6:4-6; 10:26-31.

3:8—God is pictured as giving Israel a "certificate of divorce." This appears to contradict Isaiah 50:1, where the Lord challenges Judah to show him a certificate of divorce, implying that he never divorced his people. On the level of the divorce metaphor these two texts contradict each other. The underlying message, however, is the same: Judah has been unfaithful. In Isaiah 50 the Lord insists that Judah's punishment was not because he rejected his people (and so divorced them) but because they rejected him and transgressed his laws. In Jeremiah 3 God's divorce of his people is simply the result of the people's idolatry.

The reference to a "certificate of divorce" makes clear that Jeremiah has in mind the prohibition of remarriage in Deuteronomy 24:1-4, which he had earlier hinted at in 3:1. This is also clear from the references to people and land being "defiled" (Jer. 2:7, 23; 3:1-2, 9). When Deuteronomy 24:4 talks about a remarried woman being "defiled," the same word is used as in Jeremiah 2:7, 23. The word used in 3:1-2, 9 refers to the same reality.

3:9—Judah's "adultery with stone and wood" is also mentioned in 2:27. This is a fulfillment of the prediction of apostasy in the Song of Moses (Deut. 32:18).

3:11—When the Lord declares Israel "more righteous" than Judah, this does not mean God actually looked on Israel in favor. The Lord is simply indicating that Judah was in such a sorry state that Israel looked much better by comparison. Judah is the object of the same kind of negative comparison in Ezekiel 16:47, 51; 23:11.

General Discussion

1. *The story of the two bad sisters tells us that our actions must be in harmony with our religious talk. Repentance calls for an actual turn-around in behavior. In this story what is the Lord teaching you about your life?*

Each person's view of the implications of this story may differ somewhat. But one thing is certain: all of us are susceptible to idolatry. If they haven't already done so, invite group members to recognize that in our daily walk with God we aren't much different from God's unfaithful Old Testament people. The warnings in Deuteronomy against idolatry fell on deaf ears; that's why we hear Jeremiah's constant refrain against idolatry.

It may be a good exercise to draw up a list of contemporary idols and discuss how they have a tendency to dominate in our lives. A book by Tom Wright titled *Bringing the Church to the World* (Minneapolis: Bethany, 1992) would be helpful in this regard. This book identifies a variety of gods (or idols) that we still allow to influence us today: Mars (the god of war), Mammon (the god of money), Aphrodite (the goddess of erotic love), Gaia (the earth goddess), and Bacchus (the god of wine). In discussing these and other idols of our time, be sure not to fall into abstract comments about our culture in general. Instead, be intentional about the effect of these idols on our everyday living. If certain gods affect our culture, we are liable to be affected personally. Discuss how the various gods make demands on you as individuals and how the Lord asks each of you to turn.

2. *The warning in this story is a serious one, particularly because Judah is shown the example of Israel's idolatry and the consequences that followed. Mention one or two warning examples that teach us about today's forms of idolatry and their consequences.*

The fact that the Lord uses examples to warn us is an expression of his goodness and grace. As group members give examples of warnings they can see in our society today, they may point out parallels in the bad-sisters story itself. The Lord still uses the exile of Israel and the exile of Judah as warning examples for us today. Actually the history of salvation is full of warning examples for the church. In 1 Corinthians 10:1-13, for example, we find a description of Israel's desert journey as a warning for us. Here the apostle Paul makes clear that being baptized and partaking of the Lord's Supper are no guarantee of salvation.

The Lord may also use people or events in our lives as warning examples to us. If they haven't already done so, ask group members whether they can recall any such examples and how the Lord has used them in their lives. One question that comes to mind when we think of current examples is *How do we determine when we should take something as an example and when we should not?* Here's a safe test: real warning examples will always be in line with God's revelation in Scripture.

3. *This story's setting against the backdrop of Deuteronomy 24 (no remarriage) is surprising. What does it teach about the progression of God's revelation? What does it teach about the way in which God asks us to respond to him?*

The law, including the prohibition of remarriage in Deuteronomy 24, revealed something of God himself. But God's self-revelation is not static, remaining the same throughout history. In Jesus Christ, God overcame the limitations of the law of Deuteronomy 24. God has more truthfully and gloriously revealed himself in his Son than in the law of Moses. This message lies at the heart of the letter to the Hebrews, which consistently argues that God's new revelation by his Son is superior to his revelation by the law. The Son is superior to the angels (Heb. 1:4-2:18), to Moses (3:1-4:13), and to Aaron (4:14-7:28). Similarly, the work of the Son in the new covenant is also superior to the sacrificial system of the old covenant (8:1-10:39).

One of the consequences of this new revelation is that the New Testament teaches us to live not as slaves to the rules and regulations of the law of Moses but as renewed citizens of God's kingdom, empowered to live by Christ's Holy Spirit. We have a new revelation in Christ, and God's announcement of grace despite his announcement of divorce points to this new revelation. This progression in God's revelation may lead to a discussion about the role of the law as compared to the role of the Spirit. As the discussion develops, the point to bear in mind is that the basis of the law is love, as noted by Christ in Matthew 22:37-40, and that love is also the basis of life in the Spirit (1 Cor. 13; Gal. 5:22-23; Eph. 4:1-16; 1 John 3-4).

For more discussion material on how to respond in today's world to God's self-revelation in Christ, you may wish to consult *The Moral Vision of the New Testament: A Contemporary Introduction to New Testament Ethics* (HarperSanFrancisco, 1996). In this book Richard B. Hays proposes that we look at the New Testament through three focal images:

- community—we seek God's will not by first asking, "What should *I* do," but, "What should *we* do?"
- cross—Jesus' life of faithfulness despite suffering that led to death on a cross is the paradigm for faithfulness to God in this world (see 2 Cor. 4:11; Gal. 6:2; Eph. 5:25; Phil. 3:10).
- new creation—the church embodies the power of the resurrection in the midst of a not-yet-redeemed world. The church struggles with the tension between the "already" and the "not yet" of God's kingdom (see Rom. 8:22-23; 2 Cor. 3:18).

4. *What do you think of the statement that "scaring people into heaven doesn't work"?*

One possible answer to this question could take the story of the two bad sisters and conclude that God did use Jeremiah to scare people into heaven. But you and your group may wish to discuss whether this is actually what Jeremiah did. Is warning against the consequences of one's actions the same as scaring someone into heaven? It cannot be denied that, particularly in the Old Testament, the Lord does threaten with the curse of the covenant. Nonetheless, you may wish to challenge group members to look at the verses following the story of the two sisters, where the Lord continues to call back his divorced wife, Israel. Already here we can see the Lord looking beyond the curse of the exile and holding out the blessing of renewal in Christ. Promises and threats will have a place as long as we embody "the power of the resurrection in the midst of a not-yet redeemed world," states Richard B. Hays. In the end, however, it is a personal relationship with Christ, made possible by the Savior and empowered by his Spirit, that motivates us.

Ideas for Small Groups

Opening (5-10 minutes)

Pray—Open your meeting together in prayer, praising God as the one who has taken his people for his bride. Ask the Lord to be in your midst with his Spirit and to use your discussion of this lesson to lead you to turn to him, confessing any sins you may need to repent of.

Share—Some group members may wish to mention some of the ways in which they have worked on the goals they set in lesson 1.

Focus—Throughout this lesson try to stay focused on the question *In what ways is the Lord calling me to turn to him in repentance?*

Growing (35-50 minutes)

Read (Optional)

You may find it helpful to read together Jeremiah 3:1-18.

Discuss

Look through the General Discussion questions. Question 1 will help set the stage for discussing the following process questions. If there's time, you may wish to choose from among the other questions to broaden your discussion.

On God's call for me to turn around:

- What has your study of this passage taught you about areas in your life in which you need to turn around? (Challenge yourself to ask for God's help in these areas daily.)
- Are there ways in which we as a church run the danger of refusing to turn from idolatry? If so, give an example or two. How should we be dealing with these faults?
- Mention one or two ways in which your church can bring to the world the message that there is a need to turn around.

Goalsetting (5 minutes)

Try to work on the following goal in the coming week:

- I want to listen to and act upon the Lord's call for me to turn. Specifically I want to do this as follows:

Closing (5-10 minutes)

Preparing for Prayer

Several people in your group may have prayer requests. Encourage anyone who would like to share a request to do so now as you prepare together for closing prayer.

Prayer

In your prayer praise God that through Christ and by the Holy Spirit our inability to turn has been overcome. Ask the Lord to meet the needs expressed in the goals various group members have set for themselves. Also ask the Lord to help each one of you in spiritual warfare against the idols of our time. Mention, as well, the need for our culture to turn. Pray for missionaries supported by your church. Invite group members to join in with other prayer requests—for themselves or for each other. As you conclude your meeting, you may want to sing a song or two about turning to God and living faithfully, such as "Have Thine Own Way, Lord" and "Lead Me, Guide Me Along the Way."

Group Study Project (Optional)

Some or all of you may be interested in learning more about idols in our culture today and how they can influence us to turn away from God. In a local library look up Tom Wright's book *Bringing the Church to the World* (Minneapolis: Bethany, 1992) and other volumes that may be helpful. You could report on what you learn when you study lesson 3 together, focusing on false religion and deceptive teachings.

3 The Temple Sermon

Jeremiah 7:1-15

Additional Reading: Jeremiah 26

Major Upheaval

Jeremiah preached his temple sermon (also recorded in chap. 26) at a time when Judah had just been through a major upheaval. The great world power Assyria had been waning for a number of years. The Babylonians had conquered Nineveh, the Assyrian capital, and the Assyrians had recently made one more attempt to retain their leading position. King Josiah of Judah had been looking on as the two empires confronted each other. He was hoping the Babylonians would put an end to Assyria's control once and for all. But then Pharaoh Neco of Egypt stepped in. He sent in his armies to help out the faltering Assyrian giant. Josiah attempted to stop the Egyptian army in its tracks, but at Megiddo the Egyptians routed Judah. King Josiah died on the battlefield, and the Egyptians marched on. Judah's defeat and Josiah's death in 609 B.C. brought Judah under the tight fist of Pharaoh Neco. For three months, Josiah's son, Jehoahaz, held the reins, but then Egypt replaced him with his brother Eliakim, whom Neco renamed Jehoiakim. Judah had become a vassal of Egypt. (See 2 Kings 23:29-35.)

Jehoiakim would turn out to be a formidable opponent of Jeremiah and his prophecies. The temple sermon, preached early in Jehoiakim's reign (Jer. 26:1), likely did little to endear Jeremiah to the king. Although Jehoiakim's officials declared Jeremiah innocent and refused to have him put to death (26:10, 16), his contacts with the royal establishment would soon become more testy.

Deceptive Words

The Lord told Jeremiah to preach his message at the gate of the temple (7:1). This may have been the "New Gate" of the upper courtyard, where the royal officials later assembled to judge between Jeremiah and his accusers (26:10). It's impossible to know whether the occasion was one of the three annual festivals, as some scholars suggest. In any case, Jeremiah 26:8 makes clear that there were enough people to make a mob lynching a realistic possibility. Jeremiah had to preach amid the worshipers who found in the temple a safe haven amid the enormous political and military upheavals of the past few years. Both the place and the time for the temple sermon had been strategically chosen.

We find a strong emphasis in the account that Jeremiah's words are actually the Lord's own (7:1-3, 11). The Lord himself addresses the people of Judah in the first person singular. Jeremiah is merely the Lord's mouthpiece, acting in line with the Lord's charge when God first called him (1:9). Ironically, during the ensuing uproar and trial, Jeremiah's speaking in the name of the Lord is the basis of both the accusation and the officials' declaration of innocence (26:9,16). Whenever people know that they speak in the name of the Lord, this enables them to speak without regard for personal consequences.

Jeremiah's language is inflammatory. His threefold "the temple of the LORD, the temple of the LORD, the temple of the LORD" (7:4) is almost bound to upset the people gathered for worship at this time of national hardship. Jeremiah calls this boast in the temple a trusting in "deceptive words" (7:4, 8). They are like false prophecy that does not come true. Anyone's trust in the temple is deceptive for two related reasons. First, it is a trust that isolates religion from life, cult from morality, Saturday from Sunday. This dualist approach claims it is possible to engage in worship in the temple while neglecting social justice and following other gods (7:5-7). While the people of Judah tread underfoot four commandments of the second table of the law and replace the Lord with false gods—violating even the first commandment—they merrily continue to worship in the temple. Second, this trust absolutizes the Lord's presence in his temple and thus reduces the sovereign God to a manageable deity who becomes subject to the whims and wishes of the people. This attitude forgets that the Lord has sovereignly chosen a place for himself and that the people may not presume upon his presence there. This attitude further assumes an exclusive position as the people of God and thus cannot allow for outside scrutiny of that position.

Misplaced Trust

As a prophet in the great tradition of the law of Deuteronomy, Jeremiah acknowledged that the Lord had chosen Solomon's temple in Jerusalem as the dwelling place for his Name. In fact, the Lord still wanted to live with the people of Israel (7:3, 7—see comments on these verses in Additional Notes below). This tradition, however, was a conditional one in which blessing would depend on obedience (Deut. 28). In the words of Walter Brueggemann, Jeremiah criticized an ideology that "claimed that Jerusalem was inviolate because God had made unconditional promises" (*To Pluck Up, to Tear Down: A Commentary on the Book of Jeremiah 1-25* [Grand Rapids, Mich.: Eerdmans, 1988], p. 74).

This misplaced trust in human structures also became a problem with the temple built by Herod for the Jews (from 20 B.C. to A.D. 64). One of the accusations against Jesus at his trial was that he had said he would destroy that man-made temple and in three days would "build another, not made by man" (Mark 14:58). Although this was a comment Jesus had made about "his body" (John 2:21), his accusers rightly perceived an oppositional element in his words. Wrapped up in Jesus' purpose for coming was God's intent to live not in a building made by human hands but in the hearts of his people everywhere—that is, the church, Jesus' body—filled with the Holy Spirit. When Jesus died on the cross, the temple curtain was ripped in two (Mark 15:38), establishing the movement of God's presence out of the Jewish temple. And Jesus' resurrected body, built up again in three days, was proof that the Jewish temple was under judgment and would be destroyed in due time. Likewise, Jesus' cleansing of the temple was an act of judgment on an institution that refused to see that God's presence there merely pointed to his ultimate and glorious presence in Jesus and the church, his body (Eph. 1:22-23). It was in the context of clearing the temple that Jesus used the expression of Jeremiah 7:11, calling that place a "den of robbers" (Mark 11:17). God's instrument of judgment on that "den of robbers" was the Roman empire, when its forces destroyed Jerusalem and its temple in A.D. 70.

Some Positive Elements

There are also positive elements in the book of Jeremiah, some of which the temple sermon itself asks us to look at. We may look at this passage in light of (1) the Lord's own assertions that judgment is not inevitable (7:5-7); (2) his prospect elsewhere of a new covenant beyond the judgment of destruction at the hands of the Babylonians (for example, 31:31-34); and (3) Jesus' holding out himself as the fulfillment of the Old Testament law and the temple (Matt. 5:17; John 2:21). In him, God has truly pitched his tent (or temple) among us (John 1:14). God has entered this world in Jesus. At the same time, the threat of judgment against the idolizing of structures and institutions forms the focus of this passage in Jeremiah. Starting with Jeremiah 7:8, the temple sermon no longer holds out the promise of reconciliation. The judgmental character dominates, particularly in the second half of the passage. Thus the temple sermon comes to us, as much today as in Jeremiah's day, with a strong sense of urgency.

Additional Notes

7:2,10—The word for "worship" (7:2) denotes an attitude of servility and submission, in which the worshiper bows down before the sovereign Lord. Similarly, the expression "stand before" (7:10) indicates a readiness to serve the Lord (see Deut. 10:8). The use of these words highlights the irony that the worshipers are not really worshipers ready to serve: rather than let the Lord claim their lives, they believe they have an inherent claim on the Lord.

7:3, 7—The NIV translates a phrase in these verses as follows: "I will let you live in this place." Using the same Hebrew consonants but changing the vowels, which are a later addition to the original text, we could translate this way: "I will live with you in this place." This translation is reflected in the NRSV ("I will dwell with you"). It also fits better with the message of the entire temple sermon, which puts in question the issue of the Lord's presence in the temple. Further, with the NIV translation, the word "place" would have to refer to the land of Judah rather than to the temple in Jerusalem. That rendering does not fit as well with the remainder of the passage.

7:5-6—The NIV uses the conditional "if" three times in these verses, emphasizing that God's living with his people is not automatic but depends on their upholding the heart of the law. The Hebrew text uses the word for "if" twice, both times in verse 5.

General Discussion

1. *Does the church today run the danger of becoming—or has it perhaps become—a "den of robbers"? If you feel there are signs pointing in that direction, give an example or two.*

This question challenges our willingness to be as critical of our own traditions as Jeremiah and Jesus were of theirs. The question may lead to some serious disagreements on how to evaluate certain phenomena that some may observe in the church. You may wish to caution the group that it's easy to make general denunciations that arise from a person's own negative mindset rather than from the church's own shortcomings. Any criticism should be in line with that of Jesus, who not only criticized Jerusalem but also cried over its coming judgment. As leader, you will do well to strive toward an upbuilding discussion. Along these lines the church must be open also for critical prophecy (applying God's Word without constructive criticism to our situation today) from within its own ranks.

2. *Are we in need of "temple sermons" today? If so, give an example of an area that should be more sharply critiqued. How should we deliver such "temple sermons"?*

The answer to the first part of this discussion question will be rather subjective, depending on the church(es), backgrounds, and dispositions of your group members. Nonetheless, in our Western culture as a whole, pluralism has become the norm. Mutual respect and tolerance receive high marks in most circles. It may be good to discuss whether such a permissive culture perhaps needs an incisive critique that takes the gospel of Christ as its starting point. Group members themselves may wish to point out areas in which our culture refuses to heed the gospel's call for social justice and the Lord's warnings against idolatry, for example. In each case mentioned by group members, ask what we might do to respond in concrete ways (for example, various forms of prayer, lobbying, boycotting, and so on). Throughout your discussion, remain open to the possibility that in various respects your church itself may need to hear some "temple sermons." Ask yourselves whether arrogance, self-congratulatory attitudes, and lack of involvement with the world are evident in your church, in your group, or in your personal lives.

3. *Liturgy is almost invariably a sensitive topic. What kind of attention do you feel the church should be paying to this "outward" aspect of our worship? Does Jeremiah's temple sermon shed any light on this question? Explain.*

Whenever the topic of liturgy comes up, there are bound to be people who feel that we need no change at all ("Why fix it if it ain't broke?"), and there will be people for whom any change seems to be a good one. The most tempting response would be for the congregation to try sailing a careful course between these two rocky shoals. But a course of action motivated by an attempt not to rock the boat is rarely a good one. Especially in emotionally sensitive areas it is imperative to be guided as much as possible by principles laid down by Scripture. Here are a couple of the more important aspects you could bring up in a discussion on liturgy: (1) Liturgy is not something unimportant; it naturally flows out of a life of worship (Rom. 12:1) and springs from a desire to serve and honor God in worship. Jeremiah's agitation over the temple worship is not in opposition to the temple or even against the liturgical practices so much as it is against the people's exclusive mindset, insincerity in worship, and unfaithful daily living. (2) Attention to liturgy that does not flow out of a life of worship but instead becomes an end in itself is a practice of idolatry, a following after "other gods" (Jer. 7:6).

4. *The Lord appears to set conditions ("if . . . then") for his continued presence among his people. Is God's love not unconditional rather than conditional? Explain.*

The history of the church has made this a loaded question. In much of the history of Protestant scholasticism there have been differences of opinion on whether the new covenant is conditional or unconditional.

From a biblical viewpoint, it should first be noted that Jeremiah's temple sermon addresses Judah under the old covenant. The book of Deuteronomy, on which Jeremiah continuously draws, presents a conditional covenant. It holds out blessings for obedience and curses for disobedience. And yet, remember, the Lord is merciful; he may punish, but as we saw in lesson 2, he holds out the possibility of repenting to receive forgiveness. God's love endures forever. Of course, this never implies that we may put God's love to the test (Deut. 6:16; Rom. 6:1). We must be faithful too. That's one of the central teachings of the old covenant, and by the power of the Spirit, faithful living is a natural result of re-creation in Christ under the new covenant (John 15:1-8; Eph. 2:8-10; James 2:14-26).

Second, with regard to the new covenant, both Deuteronomy and Jeremiah make clear that it would differ from the old in that God would circumcise his people's hearts so that they would not break the covenant (Deut. 30:6; Jer. 31:31-33; compare with 4:4). This means that once the new covenant is there in all its fullness, there will be no more conditions.

Third, Scripture looks at the new covenant as an end-time concept. The new covenant has arrived, in principle, in Jesus Christ. But it still needs to be worked out in full between Christ's first and second comings. Just as in Christ we have already witnessed the initial restoration of the kingdom and the firstfruits of the harvest of the resurrection, so we also have the beginning of the new covenant here today. Until the final return of Christ, our stumbling and sinning against him testify to the incompleteness of an unconditional new covenant.

Ideas for Small Groups

Opening (5-10 minutes)

Pray—Thank the Lord for allowing you to be together in the name of Jesus, praising him for his promise to be present wherever two or three are gathered in his name (Matt. 18:20). Ask for the Lord's guidance as you discuss Jeremiah's temple sermon.

Share—Let each other know how you have been doing on goals you've set during previous lessons.

Focus—Throughout this lesson focus on the question *How do the structures in my life hold up under the critique of Jeremiah's temple sermon?*

Growing (35-50 minutes)

Read (Optional)

You may wish to read Jeremiah 7:1-15 (or chap. 26) together. You could also read Mark 11:12-18.

Discuss

Before choosing from the following process questions, you'll want to cover some of the General Discussion questions, especially the first two.

On God's critique of our structures:

- What areas of your life have come under criticism through Jeremiah's temple sermon? Share an example if you feel comfortable doing so.
- What would you like to do about these shortcomings? Ask for the Lord's guidance in coming up with a solution in each area that needs straightening.
- Are there perhaps one or two ways in which your church could critique itself prophetically and seek to live more in line with God's will for the church? Give examples.

Goalsetting (5 minutes)

Try to work on one of the following goals in the coming week:

- The Lord has shown me areas in my daily living that need to be brought into harmony with God's presence in my life. Here's how I sense I'm being led to respond:

- I'm not sure yet how God wants me to respond to areas in my life that need his correction. Until I understand how to respond, I want to pray for guidance as follows:

Closing (5-10 minutes)

Preparing for prayer

Mention some things you would like people in your group to pray for, bearing in mind the goals you have set for yourselves.

Prayer

Give thanks that God has always made his presence known in this world: in the tabernacle and the temple, through the law and the prophets, and particularly through Jesus Christ, our Savior. Thank God also for the presence of the Holy Spirit during your discussion time. Invite group members to join in with items that have been brought forward for prayer. As you close, you may wish to sing together a song about worshiping God sincerely and living faithfully each day, such as "Now with Joyful Exultation" or "Dwell in Me, O Blessed Spirit."

4 The Potter's Jar

Jeremiah 19:1-13

Additional Reading: Jeremiah 18

A Closed Door

Most likely the drama involving the potter's jar takes place during the reign of King Jehoiakim (609-598 B.C.) before Jeremiah and his trusted secretary, Baruch, go into hiding in about 605 B.C. (Jer. 36:19, 26). As the story continues, it becomes more and more clear that Judah's king and the people have placed themselves on a path that can lead only to the curse of destruction and exile.

In chapter 18, as we noted in the study guide, the Lord told Jeremiah that his announcements of judgment and of grace were not unconditional but could change, depending on the people's reactions to these announcements (18:7-10). If we think of a doorway between God and the people in their relationship with him, we can see that the Lord's words in chapter 18 still keep the door ajar; God keeps open the possibility of turning back to him and being restored to enjoy the blessings of the covenant. In chapter 19, however, the door is closed. Judgment has become both inevitable and irreversible. This development stems not from a lack of grace but from the people's unwillingness to repent (18:12). The smashed jar that "cannot be repaired" pictures the irreversible character of the coming judgment (19:11).

This picture raises the question of God's faithfulness to his seed of Abraham, to his people Israel. Would God break his promise to Abraham (Gen. 12:1-3)? This same question lies at the heart of Paul's letter to the Romans: If the Gentiles belong to the people of God, what does this do to his promise to the Jewish people of God? Paul's answer to this vexing question is that God has not rejected his people Israel. Even though the jar is broken, God is still able to continue. Christ is the seed of Abraham, and all who belong to Christ are also the seed of Abraham, whether they are Jews or Gentiles (Rom. 4:12; see Gal. 3:29). In Christ, God has redefined Israel. He has simply grafted new branches (Gentiles) into the olive tree (Rom. 11). The old jar could no longer be fixed. But God's plan looked beyond the punishment of exile to an Israel that would include people of all nations. In the promise to Abraham it is clear that this was part of God's plan all along (Gen. 12:3). The closed door of Jeremiah 19 opens up in Christ, as God has intended from "before the creation of the world" (Eph. 1:4).

Topheth and Molech

The story in Jeremiah 19 presents Jeremiah going to a potter, who presumably lives near the Potsherd Gate, which leads to the Valley of Ben Hinnom ranging out to the west and south of Jerusalem. On the south side of the valley lay a place called Topheth (see 19:6, 13). Here people sacrificed their children to Molech, a god of the Ammonites.

Two kings of Judah, Ahaz and Manasseh, had sacrificed their sons to Molech (2 Kings 16:3; 21:6). King Manasseh's grandson, Josiah, desecrated Topheth as part of his reforms so that Molech's worshipers were no longer able to use it (23:10). Under Jehoiakim, however, the worship of Molech must have been resumed at Topheth, judging by Jeremiah's sharp condemnation of it (Jer. 19:5-6).

Topheth was not only a place where Molech was worshiped. It also was the dump where Jerusalem's garbage was burned. It was the place where fire smouldered continuously, making it a picture of eternal punishment for all who oppose God. (The *NIV Study Bible* includes the following in a footnote at Jeremiah 7:31: "From the abbreviated name 'Valley of Hinnom' [see Neh. 11:30], Hebrew *ge' hinnom,* came 'Gehenna,' [Greek *geenna*] consistently translated in the [New Testament] as "hell," the place of eternal, fiery punishment" [see Isa. 66:24; Matt. 5:22; 18:9; Mark 9:47-48].) The Lord's judgment on Jerusalem (the breaking of the jar) will mean such a slaughter that people will change the name of Topheth and the Valley of Ben Hinnom to "the Valley of Slaughter" (Jer. 19:6; see 7:30-8:3). People will bury their dead there until there will be no more room (19:11; see 7:32). In fact, the city itself will be defiled like Topheth. The city will become like the garbage dump and will turn into a huge cemetery (19:12-13; see 7:34).

The Curse of Deuteronomy

The pictures of judgment in this chapter are horrific. Jeremiah's graphic images are intended as more than a grave warning, however. He adopts the language used by the law of Deuteronomy and by the prophets who came before him. Note the following expressions, all of which Jeremiah borrows from elsewhere:

- "I am going to bring a disaster on this place that will make the ears of everyone who hears of it tingle" (19:3; see 2 Kings 21:12).
- "They have burned sacrifices . . . to gods that neither they nor their fathers . . . knew" (19:4; see Deut. 13:6; 28:64).
- "I will give their carcasses as food to the birds of the air and the beasts of the earth" (19:7; see Deut. 28:26).
- "I will devastate this city and make it an object of scorn; all who pass by will be appalled and will scoff because of all its wounds" (19:8; see Deut. 28:37, 59).
- "I will make them eat the flesh of their sons and daughters, and they will eat one another's flesh during the stress of the siege imposed on them by the enemies who seek their lives" (19:9; see Deut. 28:53-57; 2 Kings 6:24-29; Lam. 2:20; 4:10).

As you will notice, many of the expressions Jeremiah uses to describe the coming judgment are taken directly from Deuteronomy 28, a chapter that speaks of the curse of the covenant. In other words, Jeremiah is warning that Judah, by its idolatry, is calling the curse of the law upon itself. Judah's behavior makes destruction and exile inevitable.

Additional Notes

19:3—Jeremiah's words are meant for the kings of Judah and the people of Jerusalem. Only "the elders of the people and of the priests," however, accompany him as he speaks these words (19:1). They are likely intended as witnesses (see 19:10) and as representatives of the people. In 19:14-15 Jeremiah repeats the essence of his words in the temple court to all the people who are present there.

19:5—The word "Baal" here is likely intended to be understood in its general sense as a "baal," or "master," rather than as a reference to the Canaanite fertility god Baal. More likely, this is a reference to Molech, the god of child sacrifice associated with Topheth (2 Kings 23:10; Jer. 19:6).

19:5-7—These verses are similar to Jeremiah 7:31-33.

19:13—The defilement of Jerusalem, like Topheth, will probably be the result of the many corpses that will fill the city at the time of its destruction. According to the law of Moses, touching a dead body or entering a house containing a dead body would make a person unclean, or defiled (Num. 5:1-3; 19:11, 14).

General Discussion

1. The message of Jeremiah 19 is a harsh one. What could this chapter possibly have to say to us about our relationship with God?

In discussing how we might apply Jeremiah 19 to our own lives, it may be helpful to ask, "Where was Judah at that time, and where are we today, in the story of God's people?" Judah was about to call the curse of Deuteronomy—that is, exile—upon itself. Paradoxically, the Lord used this curse of the law, which came to a head in Christ, to bring people from all nations to himself. Today we are no longer at the same place in the story line. "There is now no condemnation for those who are in Christ Jesus" (Rom. 8:1). So it will not do to place the New Testament church today in the same position Judah had in the days of Jehoiakim and Jeremiah.

But this is not to say we can simply put aside the warning of this chapter as a description of an earlier stage in the story of God's people. There is no condemnation for *those who are in Christ Jesus.* But idolatry—worship of God apart from Christ—still makes people liable to condemnation today. Jesus' demands for radical surgery are still relevant today. Only by radical surgery will we remain in Christ (John 15:1-5) and avoid the condemnation of the ultimate fire of Topheth against which Christ himself warns all people. Together you and your group members may wish to look up Matthew 5:22; 18:8-9; 24:51; 25:30, 46; Mark 9:43-48; and John 15:1-10 to discuss what Jesus himself has to say about the danger of eternal punishment in hell.

At some point in this discussion, it may be helpful to remind group members that while faithfulness to God is essential for us as Christians, we can also depend on Christ and his Spirit working in us to keep us faithful and bearing fruit for God's glory (John 15:5; Rom. 7:15-8:39; 2 Cor. 3:18; Gal. 5:22-23; Eph. 2:8-10). If we hear and follow our Master, no one can snatch us from our Father's hand

(John 10:27-29). Only if we hate God or try to deceive him as hypocrites, willfully turning our own way and refusing to confess our sins and to open our hearts to his Spirit, are we in danger of closing the door forever in our relationship with God. Further, it has been said that being sincerely concerned about our salvation is grounds enough for assurance that we are among God's children, in case we are afraid that our shortcomings as sinful Christians are putting us in danger of hell. If we trust in Christ as our Savior, we need not fear the fires of hell. And by the power of his Spirit working in us, our lives will show that our love for Christ—and, even more important, his love for us—is real.

2. *Does the idolatry described in this chapter still pose dangers for us today? If so, how should we deal with it?*

The god Molech, demanding child sacrifices, is as active today as he ever was. Molech demanded sacrifices in return for his blessings. Likewise, our society often uses abortion to gain wealth and a sense of well-being. The abortion rates in North America today and in other Western nations are staggering—not to mention the way it has become institutionalized in some other nations, such as China. Apart from the example of abortion, you may want to discuss whether there are other ways in which we sacrifice our children to the gods of time, self, overwork, and overcommitment to ministry. The following topics could be discussed in this context: priority of family devotions, importance of Christian education, and time spent in meetings and/or work as compared to time spent in family activities.

3. *The Lord says he will "ruin" or "pour out" the plans of Judah and Jerusalem (19:7). God says he will smash Judah (19:11). Why would God do this? What does it teach you about your functioning as a jar being formed by God?*

God as the potter (*yotzer*) forms us all. God "formed" (*yatzar*) Adam from the dust of the ground (Gen. 2:7), he "formed" (*yatzar*) Jeremiah in the womb (Jer. 1:5), and he "formed" (*yatzar*) the house of Israel (18:6). God's work as the potter working with his pottery shows his sovereignty, his control. This does not mean, however, that God takes away the role of human freedom. God allows Judah to have her own plans. When those plans are idolatrous, however, God reserves the right to "ruin" them. Judah has the freedom to go against God's intention for her (18:9-10). God, however, reserves the right to respond by changing his original guidelines for his people. In this way, he remains sovereignly in control.

This perspective teaches us several things about our own functioning in relationship to God, some of which may come up in your discussion:

- As jars of clay, we cannot but stand in awe at the greatness of our God, who is sovereign over our lives.
- The Lord's method of "forming" us takes into account the way we react. Our lives should therefore follow the leading of his Spirit in our hearts as he forms us.
- We live our lives in the awareness that we will all one day face the Lord in judgment (Rom. 14:10).

4. *This chapter closes the door on Judah. From beginning to end, it's a message of doom. Should this message in any way be a guide in our outreach work? Explain.*

This question challenges people to think through some of the implications of the fact that this chapter does not present the complete story. Chapter 18 and other sections of Jeremiah that prophesy the coming of a new covenant make clear that this story may not be taken in isolation. It would therefore be wrong to take this chapter and make its approach a central ingredient in our message outside the church. The mission of the church is to proclaim the lordship of Christ. Part of that message, of course, is that he will come again to judge the living and the dead. Nonetheless, God's love for his world has been the reason for sending his Son into the world. That same love for the world must also be the church's primary motivation for outreach. It is never a human prerogative to close the door of salvation on anyone. As long as the opportunity is there, Christians call on others to turn around, trusting in God who wants all people to be saved (Col. 4:5; 1 Tim. 2:4).

Ideas for Small Groups

Opening (5-10 minutes)

Pray—Thank God for the opportunity to build each other up in faith as you meet together again. Also ask him, as the God who is in control of our lives, to use your discussion of this lesson to shape each one of you as useful jars for the Lord's service.

Share—Share together any progress you've made or struggle you've had in meeting a goal or understanding a particular detail in a previous lesson. *Leader:* Or you may wish to try a different sort of exercise to help you focus together on an aspect of this lesson: Invite group members to take turns telling brief stories about some item of sentimental value that has been broken or ruined beyond repair, such that they could do nothing more with it but throw it away. When people have swapped a few stories, mention that the very fact we remember such items shows that their brokenness has an effect on us. Next invite everyone to reflect quietly on how much more a broken *relationship* affects us and the other person(s) involved. Everyone should also silently ask God to heal the pain caused by such brokenness and, if possible, to help him or her work toward restoring that relationship.

Focus—During your discussion time, focus on your personal relationship with God in Christ, bearing in mind the following question: *Are there ways in which I refuse to follow Christ and so call judgment and brokenness upon myself?*

Growing (35-50 minutes)

Read (Optional)

Before moving into your discussion, you may find it helpful to read or review the potter story of Jeremiah 18 as well as the one in chapter 19. To cover the main messages here, you could read 18:1-12 and then 19:1-3, 7-11.

Discuss

First do some of the General Discussion questions (especially question 1). Then choose from among the following process questions.

On following Christ faithfully:

- Mention an example in which your life needs radical surgery so that you can be more faithful in following Christ.
- Think of one or two ways in which you could be of help to prevent (your) children from being sacrificed to the false gods of our time.
- Think of a non-Christian in your neighborhood. What could you do, in the Spirit's leading, to help that person come to know God as Lord and Savior?

Goalsetting (5 minutes)

Try to work on the following goal in the coming week:

- The Lord has shown to me that he takes his judgment—the curse of the law—seriously, and that life includes points of no return. Concretely, this means that in God's strength I plan to . . .

Closing (5-10 minutes)

Preparing for Prayer

Share some items for your prayer together. Include in your prayer requests some of the goals that group members have set for themselves.

Prayer

Pray to God as the Judge of the living and the dead. Praise him for sending his Son into the world so that you can look beyond the darkness of Jeremiah 19. Ask the Lord to renew his world and to bring many people to know Christ so that they may be saved from destruction. Invite group members to include their various prayer requests. Pray also for courage and strength that all of you may be able to submit to any radical surgery that God needs to do in your lives. Finally, ask Jesus to return soon to judge the living and the dead and to bring his kingdom in all its fullness. You may wish to close your time together with a song of confession and hope that looks ahead to that day—for example, "All Hail the Power of Jesus' Name," "Come, Thou Long-Expected Jesus," or "And Can It Be That I Should Gain."

5 Terror on Every Side

Jeremiah 20:1-6

The Key to the Story

The relationship between Jeremiah and Pashhur is central in our story for this lesson. It is a relationship that hinges on Pashhur's name change to Magor-Missabib (Hebrew for "terror on every side"—Jer. 20:3). The name change is thus the key to the story, reversing the relative positions of the two opponents and showing which of the two has the right to consider himself a servant of God.

Pashhur is Jeremiah's mirror image. Pashhur is a priest serving at the temple (20:1). Jeremiah, although he does not belong to the religious establishment of the temple, is also a priest (1:1). Pashhur is the chief officer, the chief overseer (*paqid*—20:1), whose task it is, as the high priest's right hand, to oversee Jerusalem's temple and to maintain order in its precincts (see 29:26). The Lord has appointed (*paqad*) Jeremiah to oversee nations and kingdoms, including Jerusalem and Judah (1:10). Jeremiah fulfills this task as a prophet speaking the words that God puts in his mouth. Pashhur also claims to be a prophet speaking for God, even though he merely has "prophesied lies" (20:6). As priest, as chief overseer, and as prophet, Pashhur is Jeremiah's mirror image, his "parody," as Eugene Peterson puts it in *Run with the Horses: The Quest for Life at Its Best* (Downers Grove, Ill.: InterVarsity, 1983; p. 207). The question raised by the conflict between Jeremiah and Pashhur centers on which of the two will win out at the end of the day.

Jeremiah's Humiliation

The story presents Jeremiah undergoing total humiliation. The beating and the night in the stocks make for a painful experience. More serious than the physical torture, though, is the fact that his "parody," Passhur, appears to have full control of the situation. The Lord appears to be vindicating Pashhur rather than Jeremiah.

It's safe to assume that Pashhur's prophesying is of a type consistently opposed by Jeremiah. Jeremiah's dramatic smashing of the clay jar, symbolizing God's word of judgment on Judah (as described in chapter 19) is what makes Pashhur undertake action in the first place (20:1). The type of prophecy opposed by Jeremiah consistently avoids the topic of judgment: "From the least to the greatest, all are greedy for gain; prophets and priests alike, all practice deceit. They dress the wound of my people as though it were not serious. 'Peace, peace,' they say, when there is no peace" (6:13-14; see 8:10-11). Such prophets only prophesy lies (14:14; see 20:6). Although Pashhur and Jeremiah lay claim to the same position, their messages are diametrically opposed. One of them must be lying. Jeremiah's suffering in prison seems to validate Pashhur's claim and that of the religious elite with which he associates.

After a beating and a night in the stocks, Jeremiah is released. Although the reason for the release is not spelled out, presumably Pashhur feels that the punishment has sufficiently put Jeremiah in his place. It's intriguing, however, that the entire passage does not mention one word coming from Pashhur's mouth. We only hear the true prophet speak, and he does so in the name of the Lord (20:3-4)—as soon as he is released. Apparently the flogging and the confinement have not been able to silence Jeremiah. The Lord ensures that his word continues to be heard. This word from the Lord indicates the beginning of Jeremiah's vindication.

Jeremiah's Vindication

The name change from Pashhur to Magor-Missabib is highly significant. As noted in the study guide, "Terror on every side" was the drum beat of Jeremiah's message of doom (6:25; 46:5; 49:29; see Lam. 2:22; Ps. 31:13). It was so central to his preaching that it had become something of a nickname for Jeremiah (20:10). By rejecting that name for himself and giving it to Pashhur, Jeremiah is saying not only that terror is coming from the enemies on the outside but that Pashhur himself is "a terror," both to himself and to others (20:4). His false prophecies lull the people to sleep, and the result will be exile. The terror ultimately lies not in the Babylonian attack but in the preaching of Pashhur. Pashhur's name change indicates that the true priest, the true officer/overseer, the true prophet is Jeremiah and that Pashhur is the enemy of God and his people.

Jeremiah then spells out the consequences of Pashhur being "terror on every side." The terror that will overtake his friends (20:4, 6), his fellow countrymen (20:4-5), and him and his family (20:6) will be comprehensive. The all-encompassing character of this judgment comes out in several ways:

- The word "all" occurs eight times in 20:4-6.
- Only two alternatives are described for the people, and both are terrible, a result of being "handed over" to the king of Babylon: this king will "carry them away" or "put them to the sword" (20:4).
- Four different words are used to describe all the possessions that the Babylonians will take away—"wealth," "products," "valuables," "treasures" (20:5).
- Three different words are used to describe the loss of wealth (and thus power): "take away," "plunder," "carry off" (20:5).

The description of Pashhur's demise is ironic. His constant message has been a prophecy of peace. His conflict with Jeremiah stemmed from Jeremiah's announcement of judgment. As soon as Jeremiah is released from the stocks, however, he indicates that Pashhur's punishment will be the very judgment that Passhur has denied would ever materialize. Pashhur will be exiled. Empathically Jeremiah declares, "*There* you shall die and *there* you shall be buried" (20:6, NRSV; the repeated "there" has been left out in the NIV).

Pashhur's punishment is also an indication that God himself will provide the evidence to prove that Jeremiah, not Pashhur, is his servant. The law has stipulated that false prophets must die (Deut. 13:5; 18:20; see Jer. 28:15-17). The Lord himself thus pronounces the death penalty on Pashhur as a false prophet. It was most likely in the year 597 B.C. that Jeremiah's vindication became clear to all. Although the book nowhere describes Pashhur's exile to Babylon, he was probably among the first group of exiles, who were deported ten years before the rest of Judah. A few years after this first deportation two other overseers had already served as successors to Pashhur (29:25-26).

Additional Notes

20:1—Pashhur son of Immer has been thought to be the father of Gedaliah (38:1). Pashhur appears to have been a fairly common name (see 21:1; 38:1). After the exile, Pashhur and Immer are family names (Ezra 2:37-38; 10:20; Neh. 7:40-41).

20:2—This is the first time in the whole book that Jeremiah's name is followed by the qualification "the prophet." This is additional evidence that this passage portrays Jeremiah as a true prophet in contrast to Pashhur as a false prophet (20:6).

Jeremiah spends the night in the stocks. The word for "stocks" occurs also in 29:26 and in 2 Chron. 16:10 (NRSV). The word is derived from a verb that means "to turn" or "to turn over." The "stocks" may have been a pillory or a small prison cell that held the body in a cramped position.

The "Upper Gate of Benjamin" is not the same as the "Benjamin Gate" in the city wall (37:13; 38:7). Rather, it was probably a gate on the north side of the temple, between the old and the new court, facing the area where the tribe of Benjamin settled (see 2 Kings 15:35; 2 Chron. 20:5; 23:20; Ezek. 9:2).

20:4—For the first time in the book of Jeremiah, Babylon is here identified as the enemy who will take away Judah into exile.

20:4, 6—Grammatically these two verses contradict each other. In 20:4 Pashhur is told that he will see "all" his friends "fall by the sword," while in 20:6 "all" his friends are said to die in Babylon after going into exile. The repeated use of the word "all" in 20:4-6 is a case of hyperbole (exaggeration, overstatement) indicating the extent of God's judgment and should not be pressed.

General Discussion

1. *Jeremiah is clearly vindicated in this story. Jesus, likewise, was vindicated in his resurrection. We may often wonder, though, about vindication in our own lives. How can this story encourage Christians today when they seem to experience only humiliation and little or no vindication?*

The Christian faith is not escapist in the sense that today we only have trouble (humiliation) and that in the life hereafter we will have eternal bliss (vindication). In a real sense we already share in Christ's resurrection, in his vindication (Eph. 2:5-6; Col. 2:12; 3:1). So by faith we already share in the life that Christ gives us through his Spirit. This realization helps prevent a negative attitude toward our present life on this earth. The Christian life is a redeemed and renewed life.

On the other hand, the resurrection still remains a future promise as well (Rom. 6:5-8; 2 Cor. 4:14; Phil. 3:11). Since we do not yet enjoy the resurrection life in all its glory, the sufferings of Christ will often be ours (Rom. 8:17; 2 Cor. 4:10; Phil. 3:10; Col. 1:24). So the Christian may be encouraged to bear his or her cross joyfully, knowing that it means a sharing of Christ's crucifixion and therefore also a promise to share in his resurrection. Today's sufferings are the birth pangs of the new age to which we look forward, as we groan together with the creation and the Spirit (Rom. 8:22-27).

2. *As in the case of Jeremiah and Pashhur, opposition and conflict often arise within the church. How should we deal with a situation in which two Christians—perhaps two preachers—make opposing claims?*

There are times when the truth of God's message is at stake because of false prophecy. Jeremiah experienced this (20:6), and so did the apostle Paul when in Antioch and other places he had to oppose false teachers who insisted that Christians had to follow the law of Moses in every detail, even though Christ had fulfilled the law for us so that we no longer had to be slaves to it (Gal. 2). The conflict between Jeremiah and Pashhur is similar to that of a court case in which God vindicates (justifies) Jeremiah against Pashhur. Just as God vindicated Jeremiah, so he vindicates all people who have faith in Christ as Lord and Savior, regardless of their background. As N. T. Wright puts it, "Justification, in Galatians, is the doctrine which insists that all who share faith in Christ belong at the same table, no matter what their racial differences, as together they wait for the final new creation" (*What Saint Paul Really Said* [Grand Rapids, Mich.: Eerdmans, 1997], p. 122).

Clarity in thinking is important in the church. As long as there is a common bond in Christ, different opposing claims must be dealt with in love within the one body of Christ. Justification by faith is the doctrine that proclaims the unity of the church: all who put their faith in Christ will be vindicated in the final resurrection and have already been provisionally vindicated in his resurrection. Opposing claims only take on the serious character of a Jeremiah/Pashhur conflict when God needs to vindicate one party against the other in the final resurrection.

3. *What does this story teach you about what God is like?*

This is a question that everyone in the group can give an answer to. If your group has some members who rarely, if ever, speak up, try for one-hundred percent participation by inviting everyone to respond. No answer, if it comes from the heart, will be "incorrect." A few possible responses follow.

- God does not tie himself to any particular institution or elite. He remains sovereign and free to withdraw his presence when his people leave truth for falsehood.
- God is the God of truth. He cannot stand lies, false reassurance, or false claims to prophecy.
- God is the Judge whose judgment can be all-encompassing.
- God is righteous (faithful). Because of the saving work of Christ, he vindicates (justifies) those who believe.

4. *The story of Jeremiah and Pashhur encourages God's people to trust in the Lord for vindication. What does that mean for the way you function as a believer in today's world?*

This story brings not only a word of *comfort* to those who experience humiliation as Jeremiah did. Because the Lord vindicates his servant, this story also *exhorts,* or urges, us to exercise our role faithfully, knowing that God will vindicate us. Together you can discuss your role alongside Jeremiah's in terms of three capacities, or offices—prophet, priest, and king (1 Pet. 2:9):

- as prophet: How do I confess God's name in this world and speak and live by God's Word to the people of today? (See Mic. 6:8; Matt. 22:37-40; 28:19-20; Acts 1:8.)
- as priest: How do I present myself as a living sacrifice to God? (See Rom. 12; 1 Cor. 13; 2 Cor. 4-6; Eph. 4-5.)
- as king (or overseer): How do I fight against sin and the attacks of the devil? (See Eph. 6:10-18; 1 Tim. 2:18-20; 1 John 4:1-6.)

For a helpful explanation of these three categories, see Lord's Day 12 of the Heidelberg Catechism. As you and your group discuss these three capacities, make sure the discussion goes beyond generalities and that people mention specific examples. The Scripture passages listed in each category should help to spark some thoughts on specific examples in our daily living.

Ideas for Small Groups

Opening (5-10 minutes)

Pray—Give praise to God as the one who vindicates (justifies) his servants ultimately through Jesus, the ultimate Servant, who died and has risen victorious. Ask God to be in your midst during this session and that he may use your discussion to give more and more meaning to Christ's resurrection in your daily lives.

Share—Group members may wish to share how they are doing with respect to the goals they have set in previous sessions.

Focus—Throughout this session, ask yourself the following question, and try to focus your discussion on it as well: *In what area(s) of my life does the Lord ask me to trust that he will vindicate me?*

Growing (35-50 minutes)

Read (Optional)

You may wish to read together Jeremiah 20:1-6. To note some contrasts in Jeremiah's own (in)ability to trust in God's vindication, invite two or three persons to read the following three sections, alternately: 20:7-10, 11-13, and 14-18.

Discuss

Work through some of the General Discussion questions before choosing from the following process questions. Questions 1 and 4 in the General Discussion section are important for getting to the heart of the story of Jeremiah and Pashhur.

On God's vindication of his people:

- Think of some struggles in your life in which you (may) have a hard time trusting that God will vindicate you. Share your thoughts about one of those struggles.
- Mention one or two incidents in which you have experienced God's vindication already in this life.
- Reflect on a topic that creates discussion, and perhaps even controversy, in your church. Then ask yourself, "Why is (or isn't) this a Jeremiah/Pashhur type of conflict?" In what kind of atmosphere should this topic be handled? *Leader:* You may wish to tie in the answer to question 2 with this discussion.

Goalsetting (5 minutes)

Try to work on the following goal in the coming week:

- I want to trust that God will vindicate me in some of the difficult struggles I have. In my prayers and my actions, I want to work on that in the coming week. I hope to do that in the following way:

Closing (5-10 minutes)

Preparing for Prayer

Take this opportunity to mention items you are thankful for or concerned about as you prepare for prayer.

Prayer

Address God as the great Judge who judges in faithfulness and defends the cause of his servants. Praise the Lord for being faithful in standing by his people. Ask God to give each one of you the enduring trust to believe that you, too, will be vindicated. Pray about any difficulties that your church or your group may be struggling with. Invite group members also to bring forward any points of thanksgiving or concern that have been mentioned. Ask, as well, for the coming of the great day of resurrection, when God will make all things right. As you close your meeting, you may wish sing a song of victory in Christ, such as "Alleluia! Sing to Jesus" or "Stand Up, Stand Up for Jesus."

Group Project (Optional)

You and your group may wish to get involved somehow in supporting someone or a group of people who are being persecuted in some way for standing up for the cause of Christ. Perhaps it's a group of Christians far away who are being persecuted and even killed for their faith. Perhaps it's someone close to home who is being shunned in the community (or perhaps even within the church) for advocating a justice issue that upsets the status quo. Whatever the situation is, begin your involvement in prayer, seeking the Lord's leading on how you can help or show support.

As a result of prayer, you may sense the Lord leading you to make contact somehow, perhaps through a letter or a word of encouragement, by means of a gift or "care package," or indirectly through someone of the Lord's choosing. You may learn of an opportunity to write government officials, or perhaps church officials, to challenge them to right the wrong being done. The field is wide open, and with God the possibilities are endless. He may be waiting to hear your plea on behalf of someone today. (See Isa. 59:15-16; John 15:7-8; Acts 12:5; James 5:16.)

6 The Power of the Scroll

Jeremiah 36

Additional Reading: Jeremiah 45

Several elements combine to make Jeremiah 36 one of the most well-known passages in the entire book. This passage gives some insight into the origin of the book of Jeremiah; it presents a detailed, dramatic story of the burning of Jeremiah's prophecies; and it describes these events in parallel with the account of the finding of the book of the law in 2 Kings 22.

Religion and Politics

In two places in this chapter the events are dated (Jer. 36:1, 9). The Lord told Jeremiah to prepare the scroll some time in 605/04 B.C. Earlier that same year, in the spring or summer of 605, the Babylonian crown prince Nebuchadnezzar had defeated the Egyptians in the decisive battle of Carchemish. About a year and a half later, in December 604, the Babylonians took the Philistine town of Ashkelon (see 47:5-7). This was the same month in which Jeremiah's scribe, Baruch, recited in public the scroll Jeremiah had dictated to him (36:9). Ever since the death of King Josiah (609 B.C.), Judah had been a vassal of Egypt (2 Kings 23:29, 31-35). Now, with the Babylonians emerging as the strongest world power, Jehoiakim had to shift allegiance from Egypt to Babylon, whose vassal he remained for three years (24:1). In this story religion and politics are as closely interwoven as ever.

Baruch and the Scroll

Jeremiah, unable to go to the temple himself, tells Baruch to read the scroll to the people in the temple "on a day of fasting" (36:6). When such a day is proclaimed in December 604 (36:9), Baruch reads from the scroll in the room of Gemariah the son of Shaphan (36:10). The room is located in the upper courtyard, so Baruch is able to look out over the crowds who have gathered for worship in the lower court of the temple.

Baruch has an important function as Jeremiah's scribe. And, like Jeremiah, he also has his moments of fear and despair. As leader, you may wish to draw your group's attention to this matter by looking briefly together at Jeremiah 45, which decribes his reaction to the words Jeremiah has dictated to him. When Baruch is finished writing the scroll and knows he will have to proclaim its message, he complains, "Woe to me! The LORD has added sorrow to my pain; I am worn out with groaning and find no rest" (45:3). But then the Lord encourages Baruch, assuring him, "Wherever you go, I will let you escape with your life" (45:5).

The contents of the scroll still offer Judah a way out. The Lord hopes that the people will "turn," or repent, so that he may forgive them (36:3, 7). This is an indication that Jeremiah's prophecies of judgment thus far were not simple predictions but were meant as conditional announcements.

Jehoiakim and the Scroll

Jehoiakim's reaction to the reading of the scroll is shocking:

- His attitude is exactly opposite the attitude of his officials. Unlike them, he shows "no *fear*" (36:24).
- When Jehoiakim's father, King Josiah, heard the words read to him from the rediscovered Book of the Law, "he *tore* his robes" (2 Kings 22:11). Jehoiakim and his attendants do not "*tear* their clothes" (Jer. 36:24). Instead, the king *tears* the scroll itself, with a knife (36:23—the word for "cut" in this verse literally means "tore").
- The king *throws* the columns of the scroll into the fire (36:23). Jeremiah consequently announces God's judgment that the king's body "will be *thrown* out and exposed" (36:30).
- King Josiah *listened* with a responsive heart to the threats of judgment that he heard in the Book of the Law (2 Kings 22:19). Jehoiakim refuses to *listen* to his officials' pleas not to burn the scroll (Jer. 36:25; see 36:31).
- Whereas Josiah sent a delegation that went to "inquire of the Lord" through the prophetess Huldah (2 Kings 22:11-14), Jehoiakim sends out a contingent to arrest the prophet Jeremiah and his scribe, Baruch (Jer. 36:26).

Josiah's reforms were a high point in the Davidic dynasty, but Jehoiakim's reign is obviously a low point. Faced with a situation similar to one that his father faced, Jehoiakim responds in the opposite way.

Trilogy of Judgment

Chapters 34-36 of Jeremiah, although not in chronological sequence, form a unit, or a sort of trilogy. Together they demonstrate the failure of the house of David. In chapter 34 Jeremiah denounces the last king of Judah, Zedekiah, who serves as a vassal of Nebuchadnezzar just before the destruction of Jerusalem in 586 B.C. In chapter 35 the *listening* attitude of the Recabites, a nomadic clan, is contrasted with Judah's refusal to *listen* (35:8, 10, 13-16, 18). That chapter ends with the Lord's comment that Jonadab the son of Recab "will never fail to have a man to serve me" (35:19). Here it is no longer David but Jonadab the son of Recab who receives God's promise. (For similar terminology applied to the house of David, see 33:17; 1 Kings 2:4; Ps. 132:11-12.) In chapter 36 we read the story of Jehoiakim as his father's opposite (outlined above) who, in effect, serves as the one to seal Judah's fate; this story thus completes a brief trilogy of judgment and condemnation on the house of David (Jer. 34, 35, 36).

Indeed, Jehoiakim's actions only hasten the judgments that are prophesied in the scroll (36:31). He is unable to suppress its contents. Its prophecies will come true. And in the end Jehoiakim himself is the one who loses. His son will not be allowed to occupy the throne of David, and his own body will be thrown out and exposed to the elements (36:30). Moreover, Jeremiah and Baruch remain in hiding and will make a new scroll, with additions (36:26-28, 32). The chapter (and the trilogy) thus ends with a declaration that the scroll—the word of God—has been vindicated.

Additional Notes

36:1—The fourth year of Jehoiakim was from April 605 to April 604.

36:4—Baruch son of Neriah came from an important family. His brother, Seraiah, was King Zedekiah's staff officer (51:59). Many scholars have thought that Baruch wrote many of the biographical accounts of Jeremiah. Baruch also played an important role in later Jewish and early Christian literature written under his name.

36:10—The explicit reference to Gemariah son of Shaphan is a deliberate reminder of Shaphan's role in the finding of the Book of the Law during the reign of Josiah in 622 B.C. At that time Shaphan the secretary had been in charge of the repairs of the temple (2 Kings 22:9-10). Shaphan's son, Gemariah, is one of the state officials who takes Baruch's message to heart (36:11-12) and who urges King Jehoiakim not to burn the scroll (36:25).

The room of Gemariah was located "at the entrance of the New Gate" in the upper, or inner, courtyard (see 1 Kings 6:36; 7:12). The New Gate is the same place where the officials took their seats to judge Jeremiah when his temple sermon got him into trouble (Jer. 26:10; see lesson 3).

36:16—The officials "looked at each other in fear." The Lord had been hoping for a reaction of fear for a long time (see 3:8-9; 5:22-24; 26:19; 32:39-40). In this story the word probably refers to fear of God's judgment, although this would go hand in hand with fear of God in the sense of worship and reverence for God.

36:19—The officials want Jeremiah and Baruch to go into hiding. They obviously know King Jehoiakim, who had earlier tracked down the prophet Uriah and had him killed because he was prophesying along the same lines as Jeremiah (26:20-23).

36:26—Jeremiah and Baruch have gone into hiding. Jehoiakim must not have pursued the arrest much further, because later on during his reign Jeremiah is free to go into the temple again (35:4).

36:30—This prophecy about the absence of a decent burial for Jehoiakim is similar to an announcement in 22:18-19. In the description of Jehoiakim's death in 2 Kings the text simply says that he died ("rested with his fathers"), without mentioning a burial (2 Kings 24:6).

General Discussion

1. *It often happens that people wonder why God's message does not have a bigger impact on their lives and on the world around them. How would you react in the face of similar questions?*

This is a rather open question and is mainly intended to reinforce the main message of the lesson: the story of our lives is ultimately not about the burning of the scroll but about its power. Point out that this question prompts us to go back into the lesson to see what Jeremiah 36 teaches us about the power of God's word. Already the Old Testament makes clear that God's word is an active, dynamic power that is never spoken in vain (see Ps. 33:6; 107:20; Isa. 55:11). An important element that you could add during your discussion is that God has spoken his final word in Jesus, who himself is the Word (John 1:1). We may trust that God's purposes in Christ will not fail. Still today the word of God is living and active and does what it sets out to do. You may wish to discuss some of these passages: Ephesians 5:26; Colossians 3:16; Hebrews 4:12; James 1:18; 1 Peter 1:23.

This main message about the power of God's word does not imply, though, that the impact of the gospel is always positive for the people involved. Like Jehoiakim, people today may stumble over Jesus as the cornerstone of the spiritual house God is building (1 Pet. 2:8). This does not mean that the gospel has failed. As in the case of Jeremiah, Baruch, and even some of the king's officials, God's word in Christ stands despite those who reject it.

This certainty of the gospel's triumph gives us encouragement. There is no need for despair when we wonder about the impact of the gospel. The story in Jeremiah 36 makes clear that God is in control even when his word is most vehemently opposed.

2. *In view of Jeremiah 36:3, 7 ("Perhaps they will . . . turn"), how far do you believe God's mercy goes? When could it possibly be too late to turn to God in repentance?*

God's words to Jeremiah in chapter 36, as in 18:7-10 (see lesson 4), emphasize the conditionality of the covenant. God's mercy is such that there is no sin that the blood of Christ cannot cover. Even Paul was shown mercy, though he calls himself "the worst of sinners" (1 Tim. 1:15-16). A complete answer to the first part of this question is impossible: it would not even be right to try to determine how far God's mercy goes. With God, says our Lord Jesus in reference to saving sinners, nothing is impossible (Matt. 19:26). God still gives time and opportunity now—"today" he calls it in Hebrews 4:7 (see Ps. 95:7-8). When God in his word holds out to us his grace in Jesus Christ, he truly means it.

At the same time, it is possible for people to harden their hearts to this word. There may come a time when they do not want to hear the gospel call from God anymore. One topic that may come up for discussion is the "unpardonable sin," the "sin against the Holy Spirit" (Matt. 12:31-32; Heb. 6:4-6; 10:26; 1 John 5:16). If you and your group discuss this matter, keep in mind that (1) this sin is a deliberate and consistent denial of Jesus as Savior and Lord; (2) Christ's sacrifice is all-sufficient; and (3) the very fear of some that they may have committed this sin shows that they have not rejected Christ.

3. *The Lord is angry with King Jehoiakim and the people of Judah for their unwillingness to "listen" (36:25, 31). What do you believe listening to God involves, and how can you cultivate a listening attitude?*

Listening lies at the heart of faith. Already in Deuteronomy 6:4, where we find Israel's famous confession of faith (the Shema), God emphasized this point: "Hear [listen], O Israel: The LORD our God, the LORD is one." When God's people listen to him, this involves more than physical hearing. By faith, listening becomes identical to obedience. As Klaus Bockmuehl puts it in a beautiful study on listening in Scripture, "In a profound way, and whether we realize it or not, listening is a form of obedience" (*Listening to the God Who Speaks: Reflections on God's Guidance from Scripture and the Lives of God's People* [Colorado Springs: Helmers & Howard, 1990], p. 145).

This listening attitude can only be cultivated within the community of believers, listening together to the word of God in study and in meditation. A prayerful life in dependence on God is essential for a listening attitude. If you like, invite group members to talk about what they do, or would like to do, to become "listeners" to God's word.

4. *Jeremiah 36 deals with the power of the scroll, the power of God's word. What is the role of the Spirit in this process? How does the work of the Spirit relate to the power of God's word?*

This question is included here because the lesson's emphasis on the power of the word might make some people wonder about the role of the Spirit. The question of the Spirit's role has often been discussed in the history of the church and has received many different answers. The church of the Reformation has traditionally been careful not to separate the work of God's Spirit from the power and effect of the gospel. For a brief summary of the

Reformed position, see Klaus Bockmuehl's book *Listening to the God Who Speaks* (pp. 121-33; see also the Group Study Project below). The Spirit uses the word of God to bring people to faith. Even though the Spirit is not mentioned in the Old Testament story about the power of the scroll, that doesn't mean the scroll, or God's word, has power apart from the Spirit of God. Neither may we try to identify word and Spirit in such a way as to limit or shackle the sovereign Spirit of God.

Ideas for Small Groups

Opening (5-10 minutes)

Pray—Ask the Lord to fill you with his Spirit so that the power of God's word may permeate your discussion.

Share—Share with each other how you are doing on any goals you have been working on since you began this study of the prophet Jeremiah.

Focus—Throughout this session, try to focus on the question *How can my eyes of faith see the power of the word of God?*

Growing (35-50 minutes)

Read (Optional)

Before your discussion, you may wish to read together some sections of this chapter (for example, 36:1-3, 11-16, 21-26, 30-32). If you have time, you could also read Jeremiah 45, which gives us insight into Baruch's impression of the situation he is in after Jeremiah dictates the scroll to him.

Discuss

Work through some of the General Discussion questions—especially question 1, which gets at the essence of the chapter we're studying. Then look at some of the following process questions.

On the power of God's word in my life:

- Make two short lists (of maybe three or four items each), citing on one the areas in which you observe the power of God's word today, and, on the other, areas in which you wish you would see it more.
- If the gospel has the power to transform your life, mention one or two ways in which that fact should affect your prayers.
- List one or two ways in which you believe the power of the gospel is at work in society at large.
- What could your congregation do to become more an instrument that shows the power of God's word and to prevent becoming an instrument that characterizes the burning of the scroll? Or what could your group do in this regard?

Goalsetting (5 minutes)

Try to work on the following goal this coming week:

- Since the power of the scroll (God's word) will work itself out in the story of our lives—whether for good or for bad—I want to live my life in the service of God. These are some of the ways in which I want to do that:

Closing (5-10 minutes)

Preparing for Prayer

Invite group members to share about items they would like others to mention in prayer for them.

Prayer

Give praise to God as the God of mercy, who again and again gives the opportunity for people to turn. Also thank God for guiding you with his Spirit as you have discussed the power of his word during this lesson. Invite group members to mention things they would like to bring to the Lord by way of adoration, confession, thanksgiving, or petition (requests). In closing, praise God for speaking to us and making new life possible for us through his Son, Jesus Christ. Before parting, you may also wish to sing about the power of God's word and Spirit in this world.

Group Study Project (Optional)

For a summary of the Reformed/Presbyterian position on the Spirit's role in relation to the power of God's word (see General Discussion question 4), some or all of you may be interested to read pages 121-33 of Klaus Bockmuehl's book *Listening to the God Who Speaks: Reflections on God's Guidance from Scripture and the Lives of God's People* (Colorado Springs: Helmers & Howard, 1990). You could report your findings at a later meeting, perhaps when you study lesson 7 or 9, each of which focuses again on aspects of God's word and power.

7 A Message to the Messenger

Jeremiah 15:15-21

Looking Back

It's time to go back to the beginning, to the messenger as he was called at first. With this lesson, we reach the half-way point in our study on Jeremiah. We have stood in awe at the boldness and the courage of this prophet. At times we have seen ourselves placed in the position of the accused as Jeremiah's preaching has pierced our very lives as part of the people of God. The prophet's sharp and direct denunciations, his messages of doom and destruction, were intended to shake us up.

All during that time, however, there was the sense not only that Jeremiah stood *over against* God's people but also that he wanted them to *identify* with him. It was difficult for Jeremiah to be true to his calling to confront Judah (lesson 1). He had to preach a warning of severe judgment to God's chosen people (lesson 2). And he bore the consequences of his preaching. He narrowly escaped angry mobs after preaching his temple sermon (lesson 3). Smashing the potter's jar in the Valley of Ben Hinnom cost him a beating and a night in the stocks (lessons 4 and 5). Dictating his life's work to Baruch and having Baruch proclaim his message from the Lord forced him into hiding (lesson 6). Jeremiah suffered as a result of his call to turn. And as we see him in his suffering, we can identify with him. There is not only a message in his words (of confrontation) but also in his life (of suffering).

An Understandable Complaint

The sharpness of Jeremiah's complaint to the Lord (15:15-18) is breathtaking. The four desperate commands he shouts at the Lord—"Remember . . ." "Care . . ." "Avenge . . ." "Do not take . . ."—are followed by a litany of objections, reproaches, and expressions of anger. It's amazing how the very Scriptures that reveal God can be so broad as to include the sharpest indictments against him.

To be sure, the Lord himself places a question mark behind Jeremiah's words as he responds to his prophet in 15:19-21. Jeremiah's call as a prophet has not made him immune to ill-conceived questions, self-pity, and fear. In a way, this is one of the attractive aspects of Jeremiah. He does not stand aloof, criticizing us from his lofty place. Jeremiah is a prophet with whom we can identify.

Everyone has times in which he or she screams out in anger or despair at God. As noted in the study guide, the poet in Psalm 88 sees nothing but darkness (v. 18). There isn't a ray of sunshine in the entire psalm, except that it consists of one extended cry for help from the Lord. The Scriptures present us with real life. They do not hide us from feelings of loneliness, pain, and anger. If the prayers of the Scriptures do not keep these realities away from us, should we attempt to remove them from our own prayers? Of course not. Eugene Peterson puts it this way: "We must pray who we actually are, not who we think we should be" (*Answering God: The Psalms as Tools for Prayer* [Harper-SanFrancisco, 1989], p. 100).

There's another reason to be careful in criticizing Jeremiah's prayer. His complaint does not fall into a vacuum. There are seven or eight so-called "confessions" of this nature in the book of Jeremiah, in which the prophet turns to the Lord in anger and frustration (see 11:18-23; 12:1-4; 15:10-12, 15-21; 17:14-18; 18:18-23; 20:7-13, 14-18). These confessions are momentary snapshots in a long life of fellowship with the Lord. Jeremiah's life was shaped by his Potter. Throughout his life he carried the Lord's message with him, faithfully speaking the Lord's word: "When your words came, I ate them; they were my joy and my heart's delight" (15:16). After so tasting the sweetness of God's words in his mouth, is it a wonder that he complains when his stomach turns sour (15:18; see Ezek. 3:1-15; Rev. 10:10)? In his own defense, he can truthfully maintain, "I never sat in the company of revelers, never made merry with them" (15:17). After he has so faithfully shunned both the idol worship of the people and the prosperity preaching of Pashhur and others like him, is it a wonder that Jeremiah gets upset when the Lord does not come through with his help? Both in his words and in his actions, Jeremiah has maintained a personal and intimate relationship with God. When Jeremiah utters his complaints, he does it as someone who knows the address to send his complaint to. When we look away from Jeremiah to ourselves and ask how well we know that same address, we are likely to mute our voices of criticism.

Jeremiah and Jesus

In his complaint Jeremiah begins with a confession, saying that the Lord understands him, and he proceeds with a request that the Lord would help him against his persecutors (15:15). And in the end he openly questions the Lord's failure to be there for him: "Will you be to me like a deceptive brook, like a spring that fails?" (15:18). The Lord looks to him like a little river that forms briefly after a rainfall but soon dries up, having no real base to draw from. We may almost feel like reminding Jeremiah of his own words that he spoke earlier on in his ministry: "My people have committed two sins: They have forsaken me, the spring of living water, and have dug their own cisterns, broken cisterns that cannot hold water" (2:13).

Jeremiah has a strong feeling that God has left him in the lurch. He is convinced that he has not forsaken the spring of living water—which is what the people of Judah have done—but that the spring of living water himself has acted deceptively toward his prophet. All that Jeremiah can do is cry out in a way like David, who lamented, "My God, my God, why have you forsaken me? Why are you so far from saving me, so far from the words of my groaning?" (Ps. 22:1). Jeremiah's complaint, so similar to David's here, reminds us also of Jesus' loneliness on the cross (Matt. 27:46).

Like Moses and other prophets before him, and like Jesus after him, Jeremiah mediates for his people, identifying with them and urging them to identify with him in faithfulness to God. And in his suffering Jeremiah identifies with the punishment his people will undergo because they have forsaken the Lord. In Jeremiah's suffering and complaint, then, we see something of Jesus, who suffered the full curse of his people "once for all" as the ultimate Mediator (Heb. 7-10).

A Critical Response

This passage does not teach us, however, that we should elevate Jeremiah's cry of complaint as if it were some superb form of religious expression. Jeremiah is down and out, and his complaint shows it. There's a difference, though, between *us* criticizing Jeremiah and the *Lord himself* doing that. Standing in the shadow of Jeremiah's faith life, we are dwarfed so completely that we hardly have the standing to speak out against him. The Lord, however, *can* speak out against Jeremiah's questioning of his help and faithfulness. The Lord's response puts Jeremiah in his place by refocusing his life on his initial calling.

Two aspects in the Lord's response point Jeremiah back to his original calling. First, there's the call on Jeremiah to turn (*shuv*—"repent," NIV; "turn back," NRSV—15:19). Earlier we noticed that Jeremiah called the people of Judah to turn (see lessons 2 and 6). They needed to redirect their lives back to God. They had to repent. Now the Lord calls on Jeremiah to do the same. Four times the Lord uses the word "turn" (*shuv*) in addressing Jeremiah here: "If you repent (*shuv*), I will restore (*shuv*) you that you may serve me . . . . Let this people turn (*shuv*) to you, but you must not turn (*shuv*) to them" (15:19). Jeremiah is in danger of falling into the same trap as the people by turning to them. He can only continue as a prophet if he himself repents. A prophet who is unwilling to turn cannot call on God's people to turn.

Second, the Lord makes clear to Jeremiah that if he will turn around, the Lord's initial promises will stand. The encouragement in 15:20 is a reminder of the encouragement Jeremiah received when the Lord first called him (1:18-19). The Lord uses Jeremiah's complaint not only to correct him but also to remind him of his promise. This promise is not that Jeremiah will be spared any of the troubles we have observed in previous lessons. The people and their leaders will continue to fight against Jeremiah. But the Lord will "rescue," "save," and "redeem" (15:20-21). These three verbs together form a multicolored picture of the Lord's help for Jeremiah. They are words that characterize the Lord's help for all who listen not only to Jeremiah's *words* but also to his *life*—a life that is meant to help bring us closer to Jesus' pattern of suffering in living as God calls us to.

Additional Notes

15:15—Jeremiah's comment, "You are long-suffering—do not take me away," expresses his fear that the Lord will be so patient with Jeremiah's enemies that they will have the opportunity to kill him.

15:17—"I sat alone." Jeremiah has become isolated because of the divine compulsion to speak. In 20:9 Jeremiah expresses the same sense of inability to stop prophesying.

General Discussion

1. *Sometimes people say that it's one thing for a biblical author to hurl complaints at the Lord but that we should not do the same today. After all, it is thought, we are not inspired by the Spirit in the same way Jeremiah was. How would you evaluate a view like this?*

As the illustration about Arnold in the study guide shows, telling people to keep their emotions in check before the Lord can have disastrous consequences. If there's anywhere we may feel free to speak, it is in the Lord's presence. The lesson emphasizes this point, drawing on various examples in Scripture. Hopefully this emphasis warns everyone of the danger that in our zeal we can crush hurting people by telling them they must deny their hurt before God.

You could also bring up other factors in your discussion here. Most important is that we identify with Jeremiah's complaint via our identification with Jesus and with his suffering and complaint on the cross (Matt. 27:46). Bothered by troubled emotions, people may find encouragement and strength in knowing that Jesus had these as well—and struggled through them in complete faithfulness (Heb. 2:17-18; 4:14-16). We are not alone in our struggles. Knowing that Jesus took his people's wounds upon himself (Isa. 53:4-5) helps us in dealing with our own pains and aches.

Further, just as our intellect and our will are to be Spirit-guided, so also our emotions are to be guided by God's word to us. Our emotions are not less important or less valuable than our intellect or our will. So we need not deny them. But they are not autonomous. We are answerable to God in all our thoughts, words, and actions (Matt. 22:37-40; Eph. 1:18-23).

2. *Jeremiah has eaten God's words, which apparently tasted good (15:16). Ezekiel was also told to eat a scroll with the words of God on it, and it tasted "as sweet as honey" in his mouth (Ezek. 2:8-3:3). Revelation 10:10 makes clear, however, that the outcome of eating God's words can mean suffering: the "stomach turn[s] sour." How do you square this result with the fact that God's message, the gospel, means "good news," not "bad news"?*

This question, like the subtitle of this Bible study, intends to challenge people to think seriously about their relationship with God—just as Jeremiah challenges the people of Judah, just as Jeremiah is challenged by God (Jer. 15:19; see 12:5-6). The gospel writer Mark introduces the word "gospel," or "good news," to us at the very beginning of his book. In Mark 1:1 we find the word "gospel" associated with "Jesus Christ, the Son of God." And in Mark 1:15 we find Jesus himself proclaiming the good news of the coming kingdom in connection with repentance, or turning back to God. This gospel account climaxes in five chapters that center on Jesus' suffering and death on the cross, in which he takes our sin upon himself so that we don't have to die in our sin. Lying at the heart of the gospel is the idea that we can only know Jesus as the suffering King, the King on the cross. We follow him only if we take upon ourselves the cross of Jesus and are willing to suffer with him. After each prediction of his suffering, Jesus warns his disciples about their need to suffer like him and for him (Mark 8:34-38; 9:35-37; 10:38-45).

Like the disciples of Jesus, and like Jeremiah, we may be called upon to suffer. This suffering of the Christian does not turn the gospel into bad news: Christians know they suffer with Jesus to become "like him in his death" (Phil. 3:10)—not in the sense of paying for sin or dying his death all over again (Heb. 9:11-28) but in the sense of serving God for the sake of his kingdom. It is in Jesus' death on the cross, in the weakness of the cross, that God shows his strength (1 Cor. 1:18-31; 2 Cor. 12:9-10). Even when we continue to have our questions about what happens to us, the Lord is able to use our difficulties to display the power of his gospel in us (Rom. 8:28-30). What's more, our suffering ultimately leads us to share in Christ's resurrection and glory (Rom. 6:3-5). This teaching does not mean a glorification of suffering, and it does not mean we may seek suffering. Rather, it provides us a perspective on suffering as a result of identifying with Christ, following his example of humility for the sake of God's kingdom. The good news remains: Jesus is King, and he has made salvation and new life in God's presence possible for us. Difficult consequences do not undermine this good news, and they may even strengthen our grounding in it.

3. *One thing that often gives the church a bad name is the un-Christian lifestyles of some of its leaders. Whether the problem is televangelists caught in adultery or internal*

disharmony in the church, the result is a negative witness that does untold harm to the cause of Christ in this world. In the light of God's response to Jeremiah in 15:19, how do you believe the church should react to such issues?

Jeremiah has often held out to the people God's willingness to relent if only they would repent. God's word through Jeremiah is strongly conditional in character ("If . . . then . . ."), in line with the law of God given in Deuteronomy (Deut. 4:5-8; 28:1-30:30; Jer. 5:19; 22:8-9). In Jeremiah 15:19 the Lord holds out a condition to Jeremiah himself. This is a message to the messenger. Jeremiah himself can only be a prophet if he does not fall into the same trap as the people. His lifestyle must reflect the law of God and the character of God.

This missionary theme is even more urgent in the New Testament. If we live in the new covenant and yet fail to be Christlike, it will be impossible to send out a prophetic word to the nations. Our lifestyle is our primary missionary activity, and it must serve as a foundation underlying any other missionary outreach (1 Pet. 2:11-12, 15-17; see Rom. 6:1-14). Discuss together what you may be able to do personally and locally to offset lifestyle problems that you believe have most hindered the spread of the gospel through your own life, your group, your church, or your denomination.

Ideas for Small Groups

Opening (5-10 minutes)

Pray—Thank the Lord for his willingness to teach and correct us, and pray that he will do so in your meeting through his power and grace.

Share—Share with each other how the goals you may have set in previous weeks are working out in your life.

Focus—Throughout your discussion time focus on this question: How does God want to use my emotions in situations of trouble?

Growing (35-50 minutes)

Read (Optional)

Before discussing this lesson, you could read together Jeremiah 15:15-21. Or you could focus your reading on one of several other "confessions" of Jeremiah (such as 17:14-18 or 20:7-18) and then read 15:19-21.

Discuss

Begin by doing some of the General Discussion questions. Questions 1 and 2 get at the heart of this lesson and lead into the following process questions.

On God's use of emotions in our lives:

- What have you learned in this lesson about God's acceptance of your emotions?
- Are there ways in which you believe the Lord would want to correct what you do with your emotions? Give an example or two.
- What could you and your group do to help others you may know who struggle with their emotions because of suffering in their lives?

Goalsetting (5 minutes)

Try to work on the following goal in the coming week:

- Since God wants to use my emotions in his service, I want to respond to his call to turn to him. Here are some ways in which I want to do this:

Closing (5-10 minutes)

Preparing for Prayer

Mention items you would like group members to mention for you in prayer. Also mention any goals you have set for yourself.

Prayer

Give praise to God, who has made each of us a person with a mind, will, and emotions, reflecting his own image. Ask God that in your response to his call you may be Christlike in every way, including the way you deal with your emotions. Thank God for the protection he has offered as you respond to his call. Also invite group members to join in with prayer requests mentioned earlier. If you like, join together in song to praise God for his sovereignty despite struggles we may face at times—for example, "When Peace Like a River" or "Blessed Assurance: Jesus Is Mine."

8 Two Baskets of Figs

Jeremiah 24

Countdown to Destruction

Jeremiah 24 places us in the period between the first deportation of exiles from Judah to Babylon in 597 B.C. and the second deportation in 587 B.C. Jeremiah had prophesied many of his messages during the reign of King Jehoiakim (609-598 B.C.) before the first deportation. In those years Jeremiah delivered his temple sermon (chap. 7, 26), smashed the potter's jar in the Valley of Ben Hinnom (chap. 19), and had his confrontation with Pashhur (20:1-6). And Jehoiakim was the king who had burned the prophetic scroll (Jer. 36). Jehoiakim had initially been Egypt's vassal, but after Nebuchadnezzar of Babylon defeated the Egyptians at Carchemish in 605 B.C., Jehoiakim allied with (or became a vassal of) Babylon for a three-year period (605-02 B.C.; see lesson 6). Then, in the last few years of his reign, Jehoiakim rebelled against Babylon (2 Kings 24:1). So Nebuchadnezzar sent his army to force Judah to submit to him. Jehoiakim, however, seems to have died before the Babylonians appeared at his gates. Some commentators suggest that he may have been killed in raids by neighboring nations that were also occurring at this time. His son, Jehoiachin, was crowned king but was only in power for three months (from the end of 598 to the beginning of 597 B.C.). Nebuchadnezzar then captured Jehoiachin and took him to Babylon, along with his mother, Nehushta, his attendants, nobles, officials, craftsmen, and artisans (2 Kings 24:10-16; Jer. 24:1). In effect, the Babylonians removed the upper levels of society so that Judah would no longer have the ability to defect from her overlord.

With Judah's king deported, the Babylonians appointed Jehoiachin's uncle, Mattaniah, as king. We will meet Mattaniah later in this study as Zedekiah, the name his Babylonian overlords gave him. Zedekiah was the third son of the godly King Josiah and was therefore a brother of Jehoiakim and an uncle of Jehoiachin (see 2 Kings 24:17; 1 Chron. 3:15; Jer. 1:3). The Babylonians may have appointed Zedekiah as king because of his poor leadership abilities. He would prove to be an oscillating figure, precisely the sort of person the Babylonians wanted to see on the throne in Judah. During his reign Jerusalem would finally be destroyed and Judah's existence as a nation would come to an end.

Unexpected Role Reversal

As the Lord shows Jeremiah his vision, Jerusalem is not yet destroyed. With some of the people of Judah exiled to Babylon and others surviving in Jerusalem, two distinct Jewish communities begin to develop. They are symbolically represented as two baskets of figs, with one basket containing "very good figs" and the other "very poor figs" (24:2). The sharp difference between the two baskets is emphasized. Note that there are also two descriptions of the baskets of figs: one when Jeremiah tells his readers directly what he saw in his vision (24:2), and another when he answers the Lord, telling him what he sees (24:3). The difference in quality between the two baskets is obviously important.

As noted in the study guide, the application would seem straightforward enough: those who have stayed behind in Judah must be the good figs, and the deportees must be the bad ones, right? After all, the Lord has spared the former and punished the latter. His blessing appears intended for the people in Judah, and his curse for those deported to Babylon. But the shocking truth in this chapter is that the identity of the two baskets of figs is opposite from what is expected. The remainder of the chapter is a description of the exiles as the good figs (24:4-7) and the survivors from Jerusalem as the bad figs (24:8-10).

The reason for this unexpected reversal does not lie in the good behavior or the wonderful religiosity of the exiles. In the first place, their banishment to Babylon is well-deserved. The Lord himself has sent them there ("the exiles . . . whom *I* sent away"—24:5). In the second place, the change of heart in the exiles is only mentioned at the end of the paragraph (24:7). The Lord's free grace is prominently displayed at the very beginning: "Like these good figs, I regard as good the exiles from Judah" (24:5). This is not to say that the return from exile—the set-up of a new covenant—would take place without a moral change on the part of the people. And this change would be initiated by God alone. God's free forgiveness and his gift of a new heart are both *new covenant* promises. They will *both* materialize when God decides to have mercy on his people by establishing a new covenant.

The Blessing and Curse of the Covenant

The description of what the Lord will do for his exiled people makes clear that the establishment of a new covenant is in view. The Lord will *build up* and *plant* rather than *tear down* and *uproot.* With these words God picks up on the terms he initially used to describe Jeremiah's calling; the Lord has been *tearing down* and *uprooting* his people (see 1:10). The exilic community may know, however, that this curse of the law is followed by the blessing of a new covenant, which consists of *building up* and *planting.* Further, the twice-mentioned promise of a "heart" to know the Lord (24:7) also shows that a new covenant is in view. The Lord has pleaded with his people to circumcise their hearts (4:4). Even though their failure to listen to this plea has resulted in exile, a new covenant will put an end to the exile, because it will come with the gift of a new heart (31:33). Finally, the statement "They will be my people, and I will be their God" (24:7) is a stereotyped expression of the future restoration of an intimate covenant relationship (see Additional Notes below at 24:7). All of this makes clear that the later return from exile (under King Cyrus of Persia in 538 B.C.—see Jer. 25:12-14) hardly means an end to the exile. The real end to the exile, the true fulfillment of this vision of the good figs, will come with the coming of Jesus Christ, the one who will bring about the new covenant prophesied by Jeremiah.

The survivors remaining in Judah, on the other hand, are the "poor figs, which are so bad they cannot be eaten" (24:8). They may think they have escaped the curse of the covenant, but they are wrong. The curse of the law may not have reached them yet, but it will. Again, the Lord uses well-known covenant language to express the curse awaiting those who have survived the Babylonian attack of 597 B.C. The Lord says, "I will make them abhorrent and an offense to all the kingdoms of the earth, a reproach and a byword, an object of ridicule and cursing, wherever I banish them. I will send the sword, famine and plague against them until they are destroyed from the land I gave to them and their fathers" (24:9-10). Hearing such language, the survivors cannot help being reminded of the curses announced in the law (Lev. 26; Deut. 28).

The law has seemed to give the survivors in Judah a clean slate. But the vision of the two baskets of figs shows that a true understanding of the covenant always turns one's false security upside down. Those who have felt so confident in their status as God's covenant community that they think the curse cannot come down on them anymore will undergo that very punishment. The end of the exile, forgiveness of sins, a new heart, the presence of God—in short, the new covenant—all this is for those who know they are in desperate need of God's mercy, which will come, as we know, in Christ.

Additional Notes

24:1—It is not completely clear who the "artisans" are who are mentioned in this verse. The listing of this word alongside the word "craftsmen" suggests a similar type of vocation. Therefore, the word has sometimes been translated as "smiths." Another possible meaning, though, is "prisoners" or "hostages."

The two baskets are "placed" in front of the temple. The verb for "placed" (*yahad*) is also used in connection with the tabernacle as the tent of "meeting" (*yahad*), where the Lord meets (*yahad*) with his people (Ex. 25:22; 29:42-43; 30:6, 36; Num. 17:4). The most likely interpretation of the two baskets of figs being "placed" (*yahad*) before the temple seems to be that the Lord has summoned them so that they can meet in his presence at the temple, as noted in the study guide.

24:2—The good figs are "like those that ripen early." There are two different crops of figs in Palestine. The early harvest is around June, the second one around August.

24:6—The images taken from construction and agriculture are used repeatedly in Jeremiah to refer to the twin theme of judgment and restoration (1:10; 2:21; 12:14-17; 18:7-9; 31:4-5, 28, 40; 32:41; 33:7; 42:10).

24:6-7—The Lord will bring his people back, will return (*shuv*) them (24:6). The people also will return (*shuv*) to the Lord (24:7). There's a reciprocal relationship here. The return from exile goes hand in hand with a return (repentance) of the people.

24:7—"They will be my people, and I will be their God" is an expression that first described God's relationship with his people in the old covenant of Sinai (Ex. 6:7;

19:5; Lev. 26:12; Deut. 7:6; 26:17-18; 29:13; Ps. 95:7; Isa. 51:16). Jeremiah uses it seven times, usually referring to the coming of a new covenant (7:23; 11:4; 24:7; 30:22; 31:1, 33; 32:38). The expression is also used elsewhere in the prophets (Ezek. 11:20; 14:11; 34:30-31; 36:28; 37:23, 27; Hos. 2:23; Zech. 8:8; 13:9). For New Testament references, see 2 Cor. 6:16; Heb. 8:10; 1 Pet. 2:10; Rev. 21:3.

24:8—It appears that a number of people have left Judah for Egypt. Opinions differ as to when they may have taken refuge in Egypt (see Jer. 41:16-43:13).

24:10—For the expression "sword, famine, and plague," see also 14:12; 21:7, 9; 27:8, 13; 29:17-18; 32:24, 36 (see lesson 12); 34:17; 38:2 (see lesson 11); 42:17, 22; 44:13. This phrase refers back to Leviticus 26:23-26.

General Discussion

1. *The vision of the two baskets of figs presents us with a role reversal. With this vision in mind, how should we today identify and evaluate our own position before God?*

Already in the Old Testament law the Lord had a special concern for the poor, for the fatherless and widowed, and for the aliens in the land. This special concern is clear in the writings of the prophets as well. In the fullness of time it also comes out with great force in Mary's song (Luke 1:46-55). The gospel writers, particularly Luke, display Jesus' concern for the lost. His parables repeatedly illustrate God's unexpected reversal of roles and his concern for those who have nowhere to turn. Jesus' table fellowship with "tax collectors and 'sinners,'" for example, is a constant source of irritation to the teachers of the law and the Pharisees (Luke 5:30; 7:34, 39; 15:2; 19:7). A reversal of roles also comes out in Jesus' constant warning to the people of Israel that judgment will fall on God's unrepentant people, while the Gentiles will join in the kingdom of God. This theme is found especially in the gospel of Matthew (Matt. 3:9-10; 8:11-12; 15:21-28; 21:18-19; 24:1-2).

Throughout the Scriptures there is a critique from within, whether it comes from the law, from the prophets, or from Jesus himself. It's a critique that insists that one's standing before God can never be taken for granted, as if it were an inalienable, automatic right. Each one of us has a constant need to repent and turn to Jesus as the only one who gives salvation and blessing to his people (Rom. 7:7-8:4).

2. *If it's possible to divide the figs into good and bad, doesn't that mean that by doing good we can earn God's covenant blessing? Or if that's not so, explain how you think we should look at our role in relation to God's role in the covenant.*

The critique from within, mentioned in the previous discussion question, should not lead to a fearful questioning of whether we are good enough to belong to the new covenant people of God. The passage we're reflecting on does not teach the fearful uncertainty that comes with a constant internal search for the marks of a true Christian. This passage merely shows that God himself will end the exile. *God* will regard the exiles as good. *God's* eyes will watch over them for their good. *God* will bring them back. *God* will build them up and plant them. *God* will give them a heart to know him. In Christ, God himself brings restoration for his people. The new covenant blessings cannot be earned. In Christ, God himself brings about these blessings. Therefore, those who have faith in Christ share in this new covenant renewal, along with its blessings. Our Scripture for this lesson should thus drive us away from our own self-righteousness and pretensions to acknowledge our need for Jesus as the one who brings all exile to an end.

This does not mean that our works do not matter. Too often, especially among people in Reformed churches, the New Testament's doctrine of justification has been read through the grid of a faith-versus-works theology. This is understandable, considering the burdens that pressed upon the young Martin Luther. However, the Pharisees in the time of Jesus and the Judaizing detractors of Paul can hardly be compared to Luther's opponents in the sixteenth century. The problem surfacing in the New Testament is similar to the one presented in the vision of the two baskets of figs: the assumption that one has a good relationship with God merely because one belongs to a certain group of people. As N. T. Wright puts it in his insightful book, *What Saint Paul Really Said* (Grand Rapids, Mich.: Eerdmans, 1997), "The Pauline doctrine of justification by faith strikes against all attempts to demarcate membership in the people of God by anything other than faith in Jesus

Christ; particularly, of course, it rules out any claim before God based on race, class or gender. Any attempt to define church membership by anything other than allegiance to Jesus Christ is, quite simply, idolatrous" (p. 160).

3. *What does this passage teach you about the relationship between churches of different backgrounds? What does it teach you about our attitude toward people who are outcasts of society?*

As you get into a discussion on the first part of this question, a word of caution may be in order. It is too easy to simply compare today's various denominations to the baskets of figs seen by Jeremiah. Such a simplification would argue as follows: "Just as the survivors from Jerusalem wrongly condemned the exilic Jews as being under God's curse, so today's denominations may not condemn other denominations because it may turn out that they themselves are under God's curse."

The mistake of the survivors from Jerusalem was that they did not realize (1) that the curse of the law was to be followed by the blessing of the new covenant, and (2) that they themselves were not beyond the reach of the covenant curse. This passage teaches us to look beyond the exile, and we know today that Jesus Christ has put an end to the exile (the curse of the law) and has brought about the blessings of the new covenant. Therefore, our status before God today depends only on our relationship with Jesus Christ. So when the question arises about relationships between churches of different backgrounds, the focus of our attention should be this relationship with Jesus Christ. The same should be true when it comes to our attitude toward people who are outcasts of society.

Challenge group members next to come up with ideas on how to approach a situation in which it has become clear that a church's or an outcast's relationship with Jesus is in pretty bad shape. Dare one another to answer the question that has become popularized today through bracelets and other trinkets worn by children and adults alike: "What would Jesus do?"

4. *Sometimes it is said that there are still outstanding promises for the physical nation of Israel. Jeremiah 24:6-7 uses various expressions that remind one of God's covenant with his people. In light of this passage, what do you think about claims made for Israel?*

In a world that has been defaced by the atrocities committed against the Jews in the Second World War, it is particularly important that we choose our words with care. At the same time, it is also important that we allow the Scriptures to speak for themselves. Romans 11:26 ("And so all Israel will be saved") has often been used to argue in favor of the notion that the Jewish nation, as a whole, will at some point turn to Christ in faith. Briefly put, there are several reasons to question this line of thinking. First of all, Paul looks at *believers* as the seed of Abraham—and, therefore, as the New Testament Israel (Gal. 3:29; Eph. 2:14-18; 3:4-6; see Heb. 12:22-24; 1 Pet. 2:9-10). It seems more in line with the rest of Paul's thinking to look at "all Israel" as an expression of the New Testament people of God, made up of Jews as well as Gentiles.

Further, we have seen that the blessings extended to the exilic Jews—forgiveness, an end to the exile, a new heart—are new covenant blessings. These blessings become a reality in Christ and are available for all who belong to Christ. This reality implies that references to the physical nation, the physical temple, and the written code must not be taken literally. They depict in Old Testament language the blessings that extend to those who in Christ belong to the new Israel.

This is not to say we cannot learn from the Jews about God, his people, and his mysterious and wonderful ways. Indeed, all of the biblical writers except Luke were Jewish. And our scholarship of the Scriptures today is much enhanced by Jewish insights into biblical passages. Nor may we write Jewish people off as unworthy of God's love in Christ. God loves all of his children, and his call goes out to all, for all of us are in need of God's mercy (Rom. 11:28-32). Challenge everyone in your group to answer this question for himself or herself (in line with the question at the end of answer 3 above): *How does God want me to treat Jews and other people who have so far rejected his message of good news in Christ?*

Ideas for Small Groups

Opening (5-10 minutes)

Pray—Thank the Lord for giving you this time together. Ask God to use this time to build you up and plant you, that the Lord may be your God and you may be his people.

Share—Share any struggles you have had and/or progress you have made as you have worked on goals from previous lessons.

Focus—Keep the following question in mind as you work through this session: *Are there ways in which I wrongly classify others as not belonging to Jesus?*

Growing (35-50 minutes)

Read (Optional)

You may wish to read Jeremiah 24 together before your discussion of this chapter. Or you could read sections of Jeremiah's letter to the exiles—for example, 29:1, 10-19.

Discuss

General Discussion questions 1 and 2 are especially important for getting to the heart of this lesson. After doing these and perhaps other General Discussion questions, choose from the following process questions.

On sorting out the figs:

- Are there ways in which you run the danger of elevating your position before God at the cost of others? Mention one, if you're comfortable doing so.
- Think of one or two ways in which your church or group could improve on expressing the unity of those who belong to God's basket of good figs.
- Mention one or two events in your life in which you can clearly see that God's grace was working in you to make you his own.
- Draw up a list of at least four items you want to pray regularly about because of what you have learned in this lesson.

Goalsetting (5 minutes)

Try to work on the following goal in the coming week:

- The vision of the two baskets of figs has taught me how we run the danger of judging people and situations in our own mistaken ways. This week I promise to ask the Lord to help me to change that pattern in the following way:

Closing (5-10 minutes)

Preparing for Prayer

Invite everyone to share items that they would like mentioned in prayer. Group members will want to bear in mind also the goals they have set for themselves.

Prayer

Praise God as the God of grace who always again shows mercy in unexpected places. Praise God for bringing the exile to an end in Jesus Christ. Praise the Lord for creating new hearts among you. Also ask for the wisdom of God's Spirit as you try to break down human barriers and try to rid yourselves of human prejudice. Invite everyone to present any prayer requests mentioned earlier. Pray also that the Lord will soon bring to completion the blessings of his new covenant, establishing his kingdom forever. Close by singing some songs together, if you wish, such as "Sing to the LORD, Sing His Praise," "Come, Thou Long-Expected Jesus," or perhaps "You Are Our God; We Are Your People."

9 Whose Yoke Is This?

Jeremiah 28

Additional Reading: Jeremiah 27

Who Is the Real Prophet?

The story of Jeremiah's confrontation with Hananiah poses the question "Who is the real prophet—Hananiah or Jeremiah?" The theme of this lesson is similar, then, to that of lesson 5, in which we saw that Pashhur was Jeremiah's mirror image (Jer. 20:1-6). In this lesson Jeremiah is confronted by a rival, Hananiah, who asserts that he is the Lord's true prophet. Throughout this chapter, both Jeremiah and Hananiah are described as prophets. This fact comes out most clearly when Jeremiah confronts Hananiah in 28:5: "Then *the prophet* Jeremiah replied to *the prophet* Hananiah. . . ." And we see that both of these men speak in the name of "the LORD Almighty, the God of Israel" (28:2, 14). Both the description of the two as prophets and the way in which they introduce their prophecies make clear that they represent two rival claims to being spokesmen for the Lord. Before beginning your discussion of this lesson, you may wish to challenge group members to reflect quietly for a moment on how we can know which one really is bringing the Lord's word.

Prophecy in Jeremiah 26-29

The concern about true versus false prophecy fits with the theme of chapters 26-29 of the book of Jeremiah. Chapter 26 records the reaction against Jeremiah's temple sermon (see 7:1-15). Here we read that the priests and the prophets reject Jeremiah's prophecy against the city (26:8-9). But with an appeal to the prophet Micah's earlier prophecies of destruction, the elders of Judah put in a good word for Jeremiah, saving him from being sentenced to death (26:16-19). The chapter then tells about the death of one of God's faithful prophets, Uriah, who "prophesied the same things against this city and this land as Jeremiah did" (26:20-23). The events of chapter 26 belong to a much earlier time period: early in the reign of Jehoiakim (26:1), as we noted in lesson 3. The chapter is placed here, it seems, because it fits with the theme of prophecy, which is central also to chapters 27-29.

Chapters 27-28 form a unit focusing on the yoke God will place upon Judah and her allies. The events of these two chapters take place in the fourth year of King Zedekiah (593 B.C.). Jeremiah is told to make a yoke out of straps and crossbars, to put it on his own neck, and to announce God's judgment on Judah and its neighboring countries, whose envoys have assembled in Jerusalem (27:3). Most likely they have come together to discuss a common strategy against Nebuchadnezzar, who had recently experienced various difficulties. In 596/95 B.C. Babylon had been attacked from the outside, and in the following year there had been an internal revolt. So it's likely that around this time some of the smaller nations planned to throw off the Babylonian yoke. The yoke on Jeremiah's shoulders symbolizes the message that Judah's allies will be unable to throw off Nebuchadnezzar's yoke. The yoke, therefore, represents the yoke of Nebuchadnezzar (27:8, 11-12). As it turns out, the strategy session held by these allies is unfruitful. Zedekiah is summoned to Babylon later that same year, 593 B.C., presumably because Nebuchadnezzar wants to be reassured that his Judean vassal will remain loyal to him (51:59).

After addressing the foreign envoys (27:4-11), Jeremiah gives the same message to Zedekiah (27:12-15). Finally, Jeremiah speaks also to the priests and the people, telling them not to believe false prophets who say that the articles taken from the temple will come back from Babylon. Worse yet, he says, other furnishings of the temple and the palace will also be taken there (27:16-22). All three sections of chapter 27 contain warnings against false prophets who predict the end of Nebuchadnezzar and a positive future for Judah (see 27:9-10, 14-15, 16-18).

Jeremiah's confrontation with Hananiah in chapter 28 is followed by Jeremiah's letter to the exiles in chapter 29. The contents of this letter are similar to the vision of the baskets of figs, which we looked at in lesson 8. The false prophets, such as Hananiah, may be wrong in asserting that there will soon be an end to Babylon's power, but this does not mean there is no hope at all. After seventy years of exile, God will bring restoration for his people (29:10).

Challenge, Confrontation, and Confirmation

Chapter 28 divides roughly into three parts. In the first part, Hananiah challenges the messages that Jeremiah has delivered in the previous chapter. There Jeremiah wore the yoke in the presence of foreign envoys, King Zedekiah, and the priests and the people (27:3-4, 12, 16). Now he wears it in the temple itself, again in the presence of the priests and the people (28:1). And here Hananiah challenges the symbolism of the yoke (28:1-4).

The confrontation that follows makes up the second part of chapter 28. Jeremiah agrees that Hananiah's outlook is far more desirable, but he is compelled to question Hananiah's prophecies, in line with Deuteronomy 18:21-22, as noted in the study guide. And Hananiah, rather than appealing to the law as Jeremiah has done, breaks the wooden yoke in front of all the people (Jer. 28:10-11).

The third part of the chapter reveals God's own confirmation of Jeremiah's prophecy (28:12-17). The Lord tells Jeremiah to go back to Hananiah to tell him that the wooden yoke will be replaced by a yoke of iron (28:13-14). While it may be possible to break a wooden yoke, an iron yoke is unbreakable. The nations will not be able to escape Nebuchadnezzar.

Hananiah is also soon exposed as a false prophet. Jeremiah prophesies that Hananiah will die because he has "preached rebellion against the Lord" (28:16). Because he has falsely claimed that he was *sent* by the Lord, the Lord will now *send* (NRSV; "remove," NIV) him from the face of the earth (28:15-16). The punishment fits the crime. The punishment also fits Deuteronomy's demand that the death penalty be given to false prophets (Deut. 13:5; 18:20). Hananiah, who has announced Nebuchadnezzar's downfall within two years, dies himself within two months. His death, prophesied by Jeremiah, is a clear confirmation of just who the Lord's real prophet is.

Additional Notes

28:1—Gibeon was a Benjamite town, approximately six miles northwest of Jerusalem. Its people originally joined the ranks of Israel in a strange way—through deception (see Josh. 9).

28:2—Hananiah's challenge to Jeremiah's symbolic use of a yoke cannot be taken in isolation. The challenge struck at the heart of Jeremiah's preaching. In Jeremiah 2:20 the Lord complains to the people with these words: "Long ago you broke off your yoke and tore off your bonds; you said, 'I will not serve you!' " Similarly, in 5:5 Jeremiah complains about the leaders of the people: "With one accord they too had broken off the yoke and torn off the bonds." Hananiah's entire approach is different from that of Jeremiah.

28:3, 10-11—Hananiah predicted that Nebuchadnezzar's yoke would break in two years. Jeremiah maintained, however, that the exile would last no less than seventy years (25:11-12; 29:10). Jeremiah may have used this number symbolically to refer to a long period of time. On the other hand, the period between the beginning of Nebuchadnezzar's reign, marking the first deportation of Judah (605 B.C.), and the return from exile (538 B.C.) turned out to be close to seventy years.

28:8—The expression "war, disaster and plague" is similar to the expression "sword, famine and plague" used in the previous chapter and in the next chapter (27:8, 13; 29:17-18) and throughout the book of Jeremiah. It refers back to Leviticus 26:23-26. (See also Additional Notes on Jeremiah 24:10 in this leader's guide.)

28:14—Nebuchadnezzar's "control over the wild animals" is a reminder of Jeremiah's earlier prophecy in 27:6. The whole world, in a sense—people as well as animals—will be subject to Nebuchadnezzar.

General Discussion

1. *The yoke in this story can be interpreted as Jeremiah's own, as Nebuchadnezzar's, or as the Lord's. How does this story challenge us to look at the the symbol of the yoke? What encouragement does this symbol offer us today?*

This question prompts the group to look back and discuss the main points provided in the study-guide notes. The yoke is ultimately the Lord's own yoke. This does not mean, however, that Jeremiah does not have a yoke to carry or that the yoke is not Nebuchadnezzar's. By keeping our focus on the Lord as the one who guides the military and political events surrounding Babylon and the planned rebellion against this world power, we ourselves may be encouraged in our outlook on world events today. The Lord is the one who uses Nebuchadnezzar's yoke and who has a definite purpose with Jeremiah carrying around his yoke—both physically and emotionally.

2. *In the Old Testament, God delivered his people from the yoke of Egypt (Ex. 6:6-7; Lev. 26:13). Jesus himself told us to take his yoke upon us because, he said, "My yoke is easy and my burden is light" (Matt. 11:30). Peter said we no longer need to carry the yoke of the law, which "neither we nor our fathers have been able to bear" (Acts 15:10). At first, Hananiah's preaching of grace may seem more in sync with this overall biblical picture, which emphasizes God's grace. How does Jeremiah's preaching about the harsh yoke of Nebuchadnezzar fit in with the biblical picture?*

The way God dealt with his people Israel makes clear that he wants them delivered from the power of slavery. God does not want them to be under a yoke. The exodus from Egypt was a delivery from a yoke. God then gave his law on Mount Sinai to keep the people in freedom, but because of Israel's constant rebellion the law turned out to be a yoke that suppressed the people (see Rom. 7:7-12). Compared to the yoke that Jesus places on us in the new covenant, the yoke of the Old Testament law looks like an intolerable burden. Jeremiah looks ahead to this new covenant in 30:8-9: "'In that day,' declares the LORD Almighty, 'I will break the yoke off their necks and will tear off their bonds; no longer will foreigners enslave them. Instead, they will serve the LORD their God and David their king, whom I will raise up for them.'" Therefore, even though God had set Israel free from slavery in Egypt and had called Israel his firstborn son (Ex. 4:22), the apostle Paul in the New Testament compares Israel's situation under the law to slavery, explaining that it is in the new covenant that we have become God's children (Gal. 4:1-7; see Rom. 8:5-17). When looking at the new situation of being God's children in Christ, the situation under the old covenant pales and looks like slavery.

Hananiah's preaching ignores that the new covenant will come about only through the crucible of exile. Israel's disobedience to the yoke of the old covenant law will have to be dealt with by means of the exile, culminating in the suffering and death of Jesus Christ.

3. *Jeremiah's role as a prophet was clearly vindicated by the death of Hananiah. In our lives we do not often get such a direct sign of God's approval. How can this passage nonetheless encourage us to speak up for the Lord's cause in this world?*

When we draw lessons from Jeremiah's confrontation with Hananiah, we have the advantage of doing so in the knowledge that in Christ God has made a new beginning for us through the reality of the new covenant. When we struggle in our individual lives with the question of why God does not give us a clear sign of approval, and why he doesn't make our vindication more clear, we need to keep a few things in mind:

- The emotional struggles involved with this sort of questioning are real. When trying to help each other in our difficulties, it is unhelpful to try and wipe these struggles off the table by means of easy answers.
- Jesus' resurrection means his vindication. This was God's direct sign of approval for him, and it was also the proof that the prophets' hopes of resurrection and of a new covenant had come true. By looking to Jesus, we may know ourselves to be already vindicated, together with him.
- The Lord has made clear that in the end his word will not fail (Isa. 40:7-8). When the realities in our lives still contradict the hopes of a new covenant, we may trust that the God who has redeemed his world will root out all evil from it.

4. *Jeremiah's dramatic act in carrying around a wooden yoke was an effective way to bring the Lord's message. How is Jeremiah's method instructive for us today as we communicate the gospel?*

Some people object to the use of illustrative objects and of drama in worship and in missionary activities. Their objections are usually based on the grounds that God does not specifically command such activities in the Bible and that they would therefore contradict the second commandment ("You shall not make for yourself an idol . . ."—Ex. 20:4). But these objections are invalid. They follow the principle that all activities in worship or missions must be explicitly commanded in Scripture, and that is an unwarranted assumption. Scripture itself presents us with numerous examples in which God's word is proclaimed in nonverbal ways. The present passage is just such an example. For a helpful discussion on "rules for worship," see John M. Frame's book *Worship in Spirit and Truth: A Refreshing Study of the Principles and Practice of Biblical Worship* (Phillipsburg, N.J.: Presbyterian and

Reformed Publishing, 1996; pp. 37-49). Frame also discusses the question of drama in worship (pp. 92-94).

There are several reasons to proceed with caution in using dramatic activities in worship, however. It is not easy to use them well. The demands to prepare for weekly worship often make it difficult to use such methods on a regular basis. It can also happen that the medium overtakes the message, such that people remember the illustration or the dramatic action but forget its biblical meaning. (The same can also be true of sermon illustrations.) In addition, it's also possible for dramatic presentations to degenerate into entertainment in place of worship (just as "special music" during worship can sometimes be). Finally, it will be counterproductive to use such worship methods in congregations in which many of the members will object to them.

But with these and perhaps other cautions in mind, we can still genuinely *serve the Lord in worship* through dramatic acts, attempting to give of all the gifts God has endowed us with (James 1:17). This can simply be another way we can help communicate the gospel by bringing God's "living and active" word, "sharper than any double-edged sword" (Heb. 4:12), to bear on everyday living in this world.

Ideas for Small Groups

Opening (5-10 minutes)

Pray—Praise the Lord together for sharing his word with you, and ask God to use this Bible study to equip you better to handle his word in a prophetic way, bringing it to bear on your everyday living.

Share—Share how you have each dealt with the goals you've set during previous meetings.

Focus—Throughout this session, try to keep yourself focused on this question: *How can I deal with the yoke the Lord gives me to carry?*

Growing (35-50 minutes)

Read (Optional)

You may wish to read Jeremiah 28 (and perhaps parts of chapter 27) as a group, or you could read portions of 23:16-40, in which the Lord issues complaints against false prophets (for example, 23:16-18, 25-32).

Discuss

After working through some of the General Discussion questions (see particularly questions 1 and 3), choose from the following process questions.

On carrying the yoke Jesus requires:

- Mention a few things in your life that you consider to be a yoke as a result of following Jesus.
- In what ways (if any) does the Scripture for this lesson help you in carrying your yoke?
- In light of this Scripture passage, how would you react to someone who feels burdened about the direction of your church?
- Mention one or two ways in which your church could be creative in bringing the gospel to the world.

Goalsetting (5 minutes)

Try to work on the following goal in the coming week:

- The confrontation between Jeremiah and Hananiah has encouraged me to take up Jesus' yoke in dealing with other people. I want to work on that in the following way, asking for the Spirit's help in acting as Jesus would:

Closing (5-10 minutes)

Preparing for Prayer

Mention items that you would like others to bring to the Lord in prayer, including the goals you may have set for yourselves during this study.

Prayer

Address God as "LORD Almighty, God of Israel," praising him for directing the course of history, of all political and military affairs. You may want to mention some concrete items that have been in the news lately. Praise God that he has shown his faithfulness by vindicating Jeremiah and especially his Son, Jesus Christ. Various group members may bring forward any prayer concerns or praises. Ask the Lord to fill you with his Spirit, so that you may be able to take up Jesus' yoke, which in his strength he makes "easy and . . . light" (Matt. 11:30).

10 The Shepherd and the Sheep

Jeremiah 23:1-8

Additional Reading: John 10

Chapters 21-24 form another unit in the book of Jeremiah. The common thread tying them together is the charge that the kings of Judah have not lived up to their identity as kings of the house of David. These chapters denounce every king who ruled after Josiah: Jehoahaz (called Shallum in 22:10-12), Jehoiakim (22:13-19), and Jehoiachin (22:24-30). Nonetheless, it is Zedekiah who, as Judah's last king, plays a central role in these chapters. He is there both at the beginning and at the end of this section. In chapter 21 we see him asking Jeremiah to inquire of the Lord because he is afraid of Nebuchadnezzar, the Babylonian king, who is attacking Jerusalem. And in chapter 24, which we looked at in lesson 8, Zedekiah is told there will be no future for him. He is the leader of the basket of "very poor figs" (24:2), the people who survived the earlier Babylonian onslaught in 597 B.C. Zedekiah, the weak, fearful king of Judah, will ultimately not escape the Babylonian curse.

We meet Zedekiah also in the heart of these chapters, in the most distinctly messianic prophecy of the entire book, in 23:5-6. Here the Lord announces the coming of "a King" who will undo the failures of all the Davidic kings who are denounced in these chapters. The coming Messiah is called "the LORD Our Righteousness," which, in Hebrew, is *Yahweh tsidqenu* (23:6). His name must have sounded a familiar ring to the people living at the time of King Zedekiah, whose name, *tsidqi-yahu* in Hebrew, meant "my righteousness is Yahweh." The issue in these chapters is that Zedekiah has not lived up to the meaning of his name—and neither have his three predecessors. Yahweh's righteousness is his covenant faithfulness, his "love in action." (For a clear explanation of the biblical concept of God's righteousness, see N. T. Wright's book *What Saint Paul Really Said* [Grand Rapids, Mich.: Eerdmans, 1997], pp. 95-111.) Whereas Zedekiah and the kings before him do not reflect that faithfulness (righteousness) of God, the "righteous Branch" (23:5) will do that, as his name prophesies.

The Punishment of the Shepherds

The Lord sharply criticizes the kings of Judah in Jeremiah 23, comparing them to shepherds who are "destroying and scattering" and driving away their sheep, God's flock (23:1-2). While holding them fully responsible for their unrighteousness and injustice, the Lord is not saying these kings have acted outside his control. God speaks of being the one who has "driven" the people away or "banished them" to various countries (23:3, 8). Human and divine action are thus placed side by side. Even though the injustice of the Davidic kings is responsible for the exile, the Lord himself has used the exile as a punishment.

The negligence of Judah's shepherds will come back upon them. Because they "have not bestowed care" on the people, the Lord "will bestow punishment" on the shepherds (kings). The Hebrew word *paqad* here can have either a positive or a negative meaning. The Lord uses both meanings in contrast with each other: because the kings have not "bestowed care" (the positive *paqad*) on the people, he will "bestow punishment" (the negative *paqad*) on the kings (23:2). God will pick up where the kings have left off. God will do what they have refused to do, but he will not do so in a way they are going to like. In punishing them, the Lord will fill in the blanks that the kings have left open. Nonetheless, when he *bestows punishment* on the kings, God will at the same time *bestow care* on his people. When he brings them back from exile, none of them will be "missing" (*paqad*—23:4).

The Prophecy of the Branch

Once God has brought the people back home, he will give them another Davidic king: "a righteous Branch." When the Babylonians finally destroyed Jerusalem in 587 B.C., Zedekiah's sons were slaughtered before his eyes. It was the last thing he saw. Then his eyes were gouged out, and he was taken to Babylon, where he died in prison (39:6-7; 52:10-11; see lesson 13). The line of David came to an ignominious end. The strong tree, which David's house had once been, was cut down so that only a stump remained.

To the human eye, the exile meant the end. God's promise that David's house and his kingdom would endure forever seemed clearly to have failed (see 2 Sam.

7:12-16; Ps. 132:11-12). But the Lord, who is able to raise up children for Abraham out of stones (Matt. 3:9), is no less able to make a branch sprout from a tree stump (cf. Isa. 11:1; Zech. 3:8; 6:12). Christ is the King through whom God will restore the house of David and at the same time return his people from exile.

The Prospect of Paradise

The failure of the Davidic kings to lead their people in righteousness and justice is resulting in exile. This means that Israel and her kings have failed in what they have been designed to do. God has chosen the people of Israel not for their own sake but for the sake of the world. God wants Israel to undo the effects of the fall into sin. Israel never managed to do that. The very Davidic kings, who were supposed to lead their people on this important mission, became instead their own downfall. Nonetheless, the Lord promises here that he will "bring them back" to the promised land and that "they will be fruitful and increase in number" (23:3). This is the very same mandate God gave in paradise (Gen. 1:22, 28) and renewed after the flood (8:17; 9:1,7). Through the terrible suffering of the exile, the Lord leads his people to a situation in which the creation mandate can yet be fulfilled. God's people "will be fruitful and increase in number" after all. Through the exile his people will go back to paradise.

This return will be enjoyed not only by the exiles of Judah in Babylon but also by the exiles of the ten tribes in Assyria: "In his days Judah will be saved and Israel will live in safety" (Jer. 23:6). The coming of the new Davidic king will mean the return to a united kingdom. This beautiful promise of the unity of God's people began to be fulfilled in a literal sense when Jesus was presented in the temple on the day of his circumcision. Simeon, of the tribe of Judah, and Anna, of the tribe of Asher, were witnesses of the King who would bring God's salvation (Luke 2:25-38). We can also see a further fulfillment of this promise in the oneness of the New Testament people of God in Christ, consisting of Jews as well as Gentiles (Rom. 3:9, 29; 9:24; Eph. 2:11-18; 4:4-6). The unity of God's people in Jesus Christ is proof that God has brought back his people from exile.

Such an exodus from exile must be more glorious than even the exodus from Egypt: this new exodus from Babylon will finally lead to a united nation in paradise restored. The result of this second, more glorious exile will mean that the people will no longer swear by God and his deliverance in the first exodus but will swear by God and his deliverance in the second exodus (Jer. 23:7-8). God uses even the suffering inflicted by the false shepherds to carry out his ultimate plan with his people and with the world. By means of the exile there will be another exodus, another united kingdom, another paradise. God will bring his plans for creation to their intended climax.

Additional Notes

23:1—The indictment of the kings as shepherds is a theme often used in Jeremiah (see 3:15; 10:21; 12:10; 22:22; 25:34-36; 49:19; 50:6, 44). In the New Testament, officebearers in the church are compared to shepherds (John 21:15-17; 1 Pet. 5:2-3).

23:2—When the Lord charges the kings with driving the people into exile, he is referring to the earlier deportation in 597 B.C. and to the later destruction of Judah in 587 B.C. When Jeremiah prophesies this passage (23:1-8), the final wave of the exile has not yet taken place. In prophetic fashion he pictures the inevitable situation of a future in which the exile will be a fact.

23:3—The word "remnant" occurs about twenty times in the book of Jeremiah. It also appears frequently in the other prophets (see Isa. 1:9; 10:20-22; Amos 5:15; Mic. 2:12; 4:7; 7:18). It refers to those who have survived the crucible of the exile and have returned to the promised land. In Romans 9-11, Paul maintains that this remnant consists of the Christian Jews with whom the Gentile believers have merged into the one Israel of God.

23:5-6—The messianic prophecy of these verses is similar to that of 33:15-16.

23:8—The return from exile is pictured as a second exodus also in 16:14-15 and in Isaiah 48:20-21 and 51:9-11.

General Discussion

1. *This lesson teaches us that even when human leaders fail us God comes to us in Jesus and shows that he is our good shepherd. How do you see the "righteous Branch" at work as a shepherd today (Jer. 23:5-6)?*

Jesus is our King, who has received all authority in heaven and on earth (Matt. 28:19). We cannot think too highly of his royal power. He is the King who has the nations as his inheritance (Ps. 2:8), who rules "from sea to sea" (72:8). He is also the King who subdues his enemies into submission (110:2, 6). Jesus is the King in whom the prophecy of the righteous branch (Jer. 23:5-6) comes to fulfillment. Both the verses before and the ones after this prophecy speak of Judah's return from exile. Thus Jesus is the King of his returned people, his church (Ephesians 2:19-22).

This means that my relationship with Christ as my shepherd is not individualistic or detached from history. First of all, my personal relationship with Jesus as my shepherd lies embedded in his relationship with his entire flock, with his united kingdom. The individual and the corporate, the personal and the communal, must not be played out against each other. The one cannot do without the other. Second, this personal relationship with the shepherd is only possible because Christ has brought the exile to an end and has introduced the kingdom of God. This united kingdom is what the oppressed people of God had been looking forward to for ages.

Within this context group members can bring up all sorts of points for discussion: How has the good shepherd tended his flock in the history of the church? In what ways can we see Jesus' control over the nations today? How has he tended me personally in the past few months? How has he guided our local church lately? Are there wandering sheep whom he has brought back home?

2. *The Lord first says that the bad shepherds have "driven" away the people (Jer. 23:2); then God says that he himself has "driven" them away (23:3). How do we do deal with these two statements that seem to contradict each other?*

This question may lead to a discussion about the relationship between our own involvement and God's involvement in our lives. It would be hard to believe that there's a real contradiction here. Would Jeremiah really have written down two such clearly opposing statements right after each other by accident? It's far more likely that the Lord is inviting us to reflect here on the relationship between our responsibility and his sovereign control. As you reflect together, you may wish to mention some of the comments in the above section The Punishment of the Shepherds.

It may be worth noting that Jeremiah does not attempt to solve the paradox. He leaves the two statements as they are, beside each other. This should make us cautious in our discussion. We may neither deny the freedom that people have to turn against the Lord, nor may we deny God's control over human affairs. We see similar paradoxes elsewhere in Scripture. For example, Joseph tells his brothers that they intended to harm him when they threw him into the pit but that God intended that event for good in order to save many lives (Gen. 45:5-7; 50:20). Similarly we know that when the Jews nailed Jesus to the cross, he had been handed over to them "by God's set purpose and foreknowledge" (Acts 2:23).

There are two extremes to avoid in a discussion like this one. First, it's possible to emphasize God's sovereignty and limit our responsibility, our choices, and our involvement. Second, it's possible to focus so much on human responsibility that we lose the comfort of knowing our shepherd is ultimately in control.

3. *The Lord is angry with the shepherds for not doing what is "just and right" (Jer. 23:5). Therefore, the Lord himself will send a righteous King. What does this teach us about the responsibility and role of church members and leaders?*

Jesus is the shepherd-king who brings true justice, doing what the false shepherds have failed to do. Still today he is implementing his reign of righteousness, using his church for that purpose. The leaders in the church therefore have a responsible position. Not only is it "a noble task" that people may set their hearts on (1 Tim. 3:1), but it is also something for which people should not strive too easily: those who teach will be judged more strictly (James 3:1). This is a timeless principle, which held for the kings in the Old Testament as well as for officebearers in the New Testament. It holds true for all leaders.

This does not mean we can draw a straight line from the Old Testament kings to today's officebearers. The kings had to do what was "right and just." Jeremiah spells out concretely what this means in relation to the poor and needy (Jere. 22:3, 13-17). Jesus' concern to do what was "right and just"—his love for the lost, his care for the poor, his concern for the oppressed—must be reflected in the lives of every church member today, not only in those of the church's officebearers. If the church wants to be the body of Christ, it must learn to do what is "just and right" in today's society.

4. What do you believe this passage tells you about the character of God?

This passage gives deep insight into God's character. In the following ways, we get to know him in Jesus, our good shepherd. Group members will likely come up with these and perhaps other attributes of God's character:

- The shepherd becomes angry when people neglect or mistreat his sheep.
- The shepherd remains in control of the flock as well as the world around it, even when people do not respect his will.
- The shepherd will bring creation to its intended purpose.
- In the end, the shepherd's care for his sheep overrides his anger with them.
- The shepherd is deeply concerned for the unity of his flock.

Ideas for Small Groups

Opening (5-10 minutes)

Pray—Ask the great shepherd to guide you with his rod and his staff during your meeting so that you may be fed by the gospel of Jesus Christ and find shelter with him as your shepherd.

Share—Share how you have dealt with the goals you have set for yourselves in previous lessons.

Focus—Throughout this lesson, keep the following question in mind: *What does it mean for me and the church that Jesus is the good shepherd?*

Growing (35-50 minutes)

Read (Optional)

You may wish to read Jeremiah 23:1-8 (and perhaps John 10) before moving into your discussion time, or you could focus on some passages from chapter 22 (such as 22:1-5, 13-16).

Discuss

Before doing some of the following process questions, try some of the General Discussion questions (especially 1, 3, and 4).

On our Lord's care as the good shepherd:

- Draw up a list of at least three items that show your shepherd's care in your personal life.
- Mention one or two areas in your life in which you may need to let go of some fears and simply trust in your shepherd.
- List one or two ways in which your congregation reflects justice and righteousness. Are there other areas in which your church should "do what is just and right"? If so, name them.
- Think for a few moments about ways in which this passage can help you to focus your prayers; then share your thoughts with other group members.

Goalsetting (5 minutes)

Try to set the following goal for yourself in the coming week:

- Knowing that the Lord is the good shepherd who vindicates me as his sheep and leads me in green pastures, I need to let myself be guided by him in the following way(s):

Closing (5-10 minutes)

Preparing for Prayer

Invite group members to mention items for which they want to praise God as their shepherd. They may also wish to mention things for which they are in need of God's care. They can also mention goals they may have set.

Prayer

Praise God as the great King of righteousness who has rescued his people from exile through Jesus, the good shepherd. Invite group members to join in with items mentioned during the preparation for prayer. Also ask the Lord to make each one of you more and more an instrument of justice and righteousness in the world. Thank the Lord as well for the fellowship you could have during this meeting as the sheep of his fold. If you like, close by singing a song about the Lord's shepherding care, such as "Savior, Like a Shepherd Lead Us" or "The Lord Is My Shepherd."

11 Trust in God

Jeremiah 37-38; 39:15-18

A Refusal to Listen

The drama has been slow in unfolding. To be sure, life in Judah has had its upheavals: battles have been fought, kings have been removed and replaced, and ten years earlier some of the leading elite were exiled. But such changes have seemed woven into a web that would always remain. Chapters 37-45 of Jeremiah, however, show that life is not so stable and constant as the people and kings might have hoped. The events have been moving swiftly toward destruction and ruin, and finally the web itself will be torn apart. The Babylonians will burn down the city and exile the people, just as Jeremiah has said (37:8).

The military situation presents a flicker of hope, however, when the Babylonian troops withdraw from the city. They had laid siege to Jerusalem in the beginning of 588 B.C. (52:4). In the summer of that year, however, Pharaoh Hophra of Egypt decided to challenge the Babylonian giant, presumably to keep him away from his own doorstep (37:5).

But the military situation is only part of the picture. Jeremiah 37:2 states explicitly that Zedekiah, his attendants, and the people do not "listen" (*shama*; "pay attention"—37:2, NIV) to the Lord's words. The previous two chapters of Jeremiah (35-36) already lamented the refusal of Judah and Jehoiakim to listen to the Lord (see lesson 6). The Lord wants a listening, obedient attitude in Judah's king. Only then will a national disaster be avoided (see 38:20). Jeremiah 37:1-5 shows two realities: a refusal to listen and a military reprieve. The question is whether the former or the latter will determine the outcome of events. This is the situation in which Zedekiah approaches Jeremiah with the request "Please pray to the LORD our God for us" (37:3; see 21:1-2).

Jeremiah's response to Zedekiah is unequivocal: the Babylonians will return, and the city will be captured and burned down (37:7-8). After this prophecy, Jeremiah decides to leave the city "to get his share of the property" in Benjamin (37:12). As he attempts to leave the city, however, some officials arrest him on the charge of desertion (37:13) and on the charge that his message undermines the morale of the soldiers and the people (38:4).

Three Different Characters

Chapters 37-38 highlight the actions of three main characters: Zedekiah, Ebed-Melech, and Jeremiah. Ebed-Melech is shown to be the most courageous of the three. He trusts in God and acts on that trust by ensuring Jeremiah's safety (38:7-13; 39:18). Zedekiah, on the other hand, is clearly the weakest of the three, the one who has no trust in God at all. Driven by fear, he asks Jeremiah to pray for him (37:3). He swings back and forth from one position to another, first allowing his officials to arrest Jeremiah and do as they please with him (38:5), and then giving Ebed-Melech permission to free the prophet from the cistern (38:10). Afraid of his officials, Zedekiah meets privately with Jeremiah and asks him for a message from God (37:17; 38:16, 24). Afraid that the Babylonians will hand him over to people from Judah who have already deserted, he does not dare surrender to the Babylonians (38:19).

Zedekiah is not the only one, however, who is afraid in this moment of crisis. Asked by the king whether he has a word from the Lord, Jeremiah hesitates. He has already been in the dungeon, and he is afraid of giving any more bad messages to the king (38:15). Only when the king promises him immunity does Jeremiah give him another warning from the Lord, urging him to surrender to the king of Babylon (38:17). When Zedekiah warns him not to tell anyone about the details of this discussion, Jeremiah complies. He tells the officials only what the king has told him to say (38:24-27). Although he tells them the truth—that he pleaded with the king not to be sent back to Jonathan's house, where the dungeon/cistern is (see 37:20; also 37:15-16; 38:6)—this is only part of the truth. Jeremiah, afraid of the consequences of telling the whole story, does not tell the officials that he has warned the king to surrender to Babylon.

Jeremiah's fearful attitude is understandable. The many years of persecution, culminating in the time spent in the cold, muddy cistern, must have made an impact on him. And he knows that Zedekiah cannot be trusted. Jeremiah's fears are an indication that even this bold man of faith, this "fortified city" (1:18), has his moments of weakness and doubt. But he remains a man of faith. When he does speak to Zedekiah, he unflinchingly speaks the word of God.

Zedekiah in the Mud

Two elements in Jeremiah's reaction to Zedekiah call for our attention. First, Jeremiah still places a choice before the king. Even at this very last moment, with the Babylonians close by, Zedekiah can still avert disaster. If he surrenders, Zedekiah, his family, and the city will all be spared (38:17, 20). The Lord's patience stretches amazingly far. After all the warnings Jeremiah has presented, after the many indications that Zedekiah has refused to listen, the king still gets the opportunity to repent. When Zedekiah, driven by his fear, does not do that, he himself sets the stage for the fall of Jerusalem and the exile to Babylon. God's judgment of exile is entirely deserved; the kings and the people of Judah bring it upon themselves. It is in no way a capricious act.

Second, Jeremiah presents a horrific description of what will happen if Zedekiah refuses to surrender (38:21-23). Here Jeremiah describes a vision the Lord has given him. In his vision he sees the women of the palace—the king's wives and concubines—brought to the Babylonian officials. The women face their defeated king, Zedekiah, and sing a mocking lament to him: "They misled you and overcame you—those trusted friends of yours. Your feet are sunk in the mud; your friends have deserted you" (38:22). In this song the women of the palace ridicule their king's weakness. He has admitted to his "friends"—his officials—that he could "do" (*yalad*) nothing to oppose them (38:5). The women mockingly confirm the king's weakness by saying his officials have "overcome" (*yalad*) him. Zedekiah's officials are stronger than he is. And the result is that Zedekiah's feet will be "sunk in the mud," just as Jeremiah's were a little while earlier. This does not mean Zedekiah will literally be placed in the mud. This figure of speech is used to remind Zedekiah of the reversal of roles between himself and Jeremiah. The metaphor of sinking down in the mud is a description of being in deep distress (see Ps. 69:14.)

Additional Notes

37:5, 7—Pharaoh Hophra (44:30), who ruled Egypt from 589-570 B.C., probably marched out to confront the Babylonians because of a request from Judah. In archeological digs, pieces of broken pottery have made clear that around this time the commander of Judah visited Egypt. Hophra, however, was defeated by Nebuchadnezzar, who then resumed the siege of Jerusalem (see Isa. 36:6; Ezek. 29:6; 30:21).

37:11-38:28—The events described in 37:11-21 most likely overlap those described in chapter 38. The many similarities between these two sections give strong indications that they describe the same events. Other passages in Jeremiah contain similar kinds of overlapping descriptions (for example, 7:1-15 and 26:1-6, as noted in lesson 3). Chronologically we can divide chapters 37-38 into six sections:

A	37:1-10	Zedekiah's prayer request; Jeremiah's response
B	37:11-15; 38:1-4	Jeremiah's "escape" and arrest
C	37:16; 38:5-6	Jeremiah imprisoned
D	38:7-13	Ebed-Melech rescues Jeremiah
E	37:17-20; 38:14-26	discussion between Jeremiah and Zedekiah
F	37:21; 38:27-28	Jeremiah in the courtyard of the guard

The main differences between these overlapping sections are as follows:

- In section B, chapter 38 omits the incident of Jeremiah atttempting to leave the city and gives a slightly different background to his arrest.
- Chapter 37 omits section D.
- Chapter 37 describes the dungeon as being in the house of Jonathan the secretary (37:15-16; see 38:26), while chapter 38 states that the cistern belongs to Malkijah, "the king's son," which probably means he was one of the king's officials (38:6; see 36:26). The word for "dungeon" in 37:16 is the same word translated as "cistern" in 38:6, 13, so both chapters appear to be speaking about the same imprisonment.
- Section E receives far more attention in chapter 38 than in chapter 37.

General Discussion

1. *What can we learn from the sharp contrast between Zedekiah and Ebed-Melech in our Scripture readings for this lesson?*

The story in our Scripture readings deliberately contrasts the two men (38:5, 7). Zedekiah's failure to listen and repent sets the stage for the next couple of chapters, which spell out the destruction of Jerusalem and the exile. As the last king of Judah, Zedekiah is immediately responsible for the exile. Ebed-Melech, on the other hand, trusts the Lord and does what is right, and he is rewarded with the Lord's "rescue" (39:18). The actions of the two men highlight our individual responsibility to trust in God (39:18) and to listen (*shama*—37:2; 38:15) to what God has to say to us. You may wish include other comments about these two men as noted in the above section Three Different Characters.

The contrast between Ebed-Melech and Zedekiah shows that there's a sharp line between God's trusting, obedient children and those who go their own way. However, the story also makes the remarkable point that those whom we consider God's children could turn out not to be such, and vice-versa. While in our story the king of God's people is being prepared for judgment, a foreign servant receives God's approval. This is one example in which God's grace reaches beyond national boundaries already in the Old Testament. The story may be seen as a pointer to Pentecost, when God's Spirit poured out on all nations.

At the same time, the story does not leave us off the hook. People who are confident that they are God's children are cautioned, just as Jesus cautioned the expert in the law with the story of the good Samaritan (Luke 10:25-37). God's people must always be careful to "listen," or "pay attention," to the Lord's will (37:2; 38:15). We may never presume upon our status as members of God's family as though it were automatic or self-evident. Instead, we may be grateful for being clothed with Christ's righteousness, trusting in him as God our Savior, as we live gratefully by the power of his Holy Spirit within us.

2. *Describe Jeremiah's attitude in chapters 37-38. What does his attitude indicate about the believer's relationship with God?*

As noted in the above section Three Different Characters, Jeremiah does not always stand strong in his faith. Already in lesson 7 we saw the Lord warning him that he had to turn around (15:19). The book of Jeremiah does present our prophet as a courageous figure, but not as a perfect one. When we as Christians struggle with sins and shortcomings, we do not need to despair: "If we claim to be without sin, we deceive ourselves and the truth is not in us" (1 John 1:8). The Bible does not teach perfectionism. While we are led by the Spirit of Christ to "ever-increasing glory" (2 Cor. 3:18), we will continue to struggle with sins and shortcomings (Rom. 7:15-25) until the day Christ comes and makes us complete. Invite group members to share any insights they may have gained from this lesson about their own relationships with God.

3. *Why does Jeremiah not pray for Zedekiah (Jer. 37:3, 6-8)? Should we ever refuse to pray when others have a prayer request? Explain. What does Jeremiah's refusal to pray teach us about our own prayer life?*

In the study guide we have already noted a similar instance in which Zedekiah asked Jeremiah to pray (21:2). But Jeremiah's refusal to pray for others is not limited to 21:2-4 and 37:3, 6-8. In 7:13-18 the Lord tells Jeremiah not to pray for his people because they do not listen and are engaged in idolatry. In 11:8-14 the Lord tells Jeremiah the same thing for the same reasons. In 14:10-11 the Lord again tells Jeremiah not to pray for the people because they are wandering away (see also 15:1). These passages indicate that when God's people leave him to serve other gods, and when they refuse to listen to him, he in turn will not listen to them. Jeremiah's harsh response to Zedekiah is based on the king's own refusal to listen to God.

Whether we should refuse to pray for others, however, is quite another matter. Zedekiah's refusal to listen is linked to the exile as God's covenant curse. The law had warned about this impending doom. If Jeremiah had prayed for the future of Zedekiah and the people, he would have gone against the clear teaching of Deuteronomy. What Jeremiah refuses to do is to plead with God not to bring about the exile, while the actions of the king and his people clearly call for that curse.

Our Lord Jesus teaches us that we should pray for our enemies (Matt. 5:44; Luke 23:34; see Acts 7:60). Jesus himself prayed for Peter, knowing that this disciple would deny his Master (Luke 22:32). Perhaps only in cases of open and willful rejection of Jesus Christ and the working of his Holy Spirit does one not need to pray for others (1 John

5:16; see Matt. 12:32). The difficulty of determining when somebody has committed such a sin should encourage us in our practice of intercessory prayer. If God says that he takes no pleasure in the death of anyone (Ezek. 18:32; 2 Pet. 3:9), we may pray in line with this desire of God.

Further, the situation of Zedekiah should caution us against using prayer as an emergency measure. If our lives are not prayerful lives, we can hardly expect God to listen to us when we are faced with a crisis. We can only expect our prayers to be heard if our relationship with God is marked by repentance and confession of sin and has become a two-way street (1 John 1:6-10). And even then we may not presuppose God's answers, for God's ways are not our ways (Isa. 55:8-9). When we ask in line with God's will, however, our requests will be granted (Luke 11:9-13; John 15:7-17; see Luke 22:42; James 4:3-4).

Ideas for Small Groups

Opening (5-10 minutes)

Pray—Thank God for being willing to listen to his children when they call on their Lord, and pray for openness in each person's heart to hear what God has to say in our Scriptures for this lesson.

Share—Discuss goals you may have set in previous sessions. Share together how you're progressing on those goals.

Focus—Discuss these chapters with this question in mind: *How does God want me to listen to him and trust in him?*

Growing (35-50 minutes)

Read (Optional)

Before moving into your discussion time, you may wish to read or review a few key passages from our Scriptures for this lesson, such as 37:1-8, 11-15; 38:7-18.

Discuss

First do some of the General Discussion questions (especially 1 and 2). Then choose from the process questions below.

On trusting God:

- What have these chapters taught you about the importance of putting your trust in God? Give one or two examples.
- Mention one or two ways in which we as the church today could be in danger of refusing to listen to God while asking God to listen to us.
- With whom would you identify in this story—Zedekiah, Jeremiah, or Ebed-Melech? Why?

Goalsetting (5 minutes)

Challenge yourself to work on the following goal in the coming week:

- God has called on me in this lesson to listen to him and trust in him. I want to ask God regularly to help me do that in the following ways:

Closing (5-10 minutes)

Preparing for Prayer

Share items, including goals you've set, that you would like mentioned as you close in prayer together.

Prayer

Praise God for being trustworthy and for listening to his children. Ask the Lord to keep you close at all times, so that you may not fall into the danger of refusing to listen to God while expecting him to be there for you. Pray that God may bless the work of mission and thus rescue many people. Invite group members to join in with prayer requests mentioned earlier. If you like, conclude your meeting by singing some songs like "Great Is Thy Faithfulness" and "Abide with Me."

12 Is Anything Too Hard for God?

Jeremiah 32

Looking Past the Exile

With this chapter we are again faced with the confusing fact that the book of Jeremiah is not ordered strictly chronologically but mainly thematically. The "Book of Consolation" (Jer. 30-33) mentioned in the study guide presents a ray of sunshine amid gloomy predictions of destruction and exile. Now that the Babylonians have surrounded Jerusalem, with Jeremiah imprisoned under King Zedekiah in the courtyard of the guard, and with the exile just around the corner, Jeremiah is called by God to prophesy restoration. These chapters look beyond the exile to Israel's restoration and to a new covenant (31:31-34). The New Testament book of Hebrews reflects back on the description here of a new covenant and indicates that it has become a reality for all who belong to Jesus Christ (Heb. 8:7-13; 10:15-18).

Zedekiah, the weak and wavering last king of Judah, approaches Jeremiah and questions his negative approach. Does Jeremiah not have something positive to say about Zedekiah's own fate? (See Jer. 32:3-5; also 37:17; 38:17-23.) The ensuing story is Jeremiah's response to the king. It consists of three sections: Jeremiah's purchase of a field from his cousin Hanamel (32:6-15), Jeremiah's prayer (32:16-25), and the Lord's response to Jeremiah (32:26-44). Although the Lord opens up a perspective that looks beyond the judgment of the exile, this does not mean Zedekiah will share in the blessings of the new covenant. The Lord does not undo the announcement of judgment on his people who have refused to live by his law. Instead the Lord encourages Jeremiah by opening up a historical perspective that looks past the judgment of exile on the present generation to those who are included in the new covenant, which we know has been revealed in Christ.

Hanamel's Offer

Jeremiah appears to have had some interest in the land around his hometown, Anathoth (three miles northeast of Jerusalem). In the summer of the previous year (588 B.C.), while the Babylonians had briefly withdrawn from the city to fight the Egyptians (37:5), he headed for the territory of Benjamin to get his share of the property there. His attempt to leave the city at that time had been the occasion of his imprisonment in the courtyard of the guard (37:11-16; 38:1-5).

Hanamel's offer to Jeremiah has been interpreted in various ways. Some scholars think that this cousin of Jeremiah wanted to get rid of a piece of land now that the Babylonians were taking over. He would see no future in owning land anymore. In such a scenario, though, it remains unclear how Hanamel could think that Jeremiah, a prisoner, could be interested in buying a piece of land. Alternatively, other scholars have thought that Hanamel is a poor man who wants to prevent his property from falling into his creditors' hands. Therefore he would want Jeremiah to redeem it in line with the Levitical law of redemption (Lev. 25:25-31). But the law of redemption called for the nearest family member to *buy back* a piece of land from the person it had been sold to (usually as payment for a debt) and to return the land to its original owner. Hanamel, however, speaks of it as his own land (32:7-8), so he cannot be a poor man who has been forced to sell his land.

This means we should look in a different direction to interpret Hanamel's offer. Perhaps Hanamel has come to mock Jeremiah and thus add to his suffering, as suggested in the study guide. This scenario is possible because it would tie Hanamel in with the rest of his family. The people of Anathoth, including some of Jeremiah's family members, had earlier been trying to kill him (11:21-23). The Lord had warned Jeremiah about this: "Your brothers, your own family—even they have betrayed you; they have raised a loud cry against you. Do not trust them, though they speak well of you" (12:6). With a veiled reference to the law of redemption, then, it appears that Hanamel is ridiculing Jeremiah's faithfulness to the law, making clear that he has no use for Jeremiah's prophecies and that he has no pity on him in his plight.

The Lord, however, tells Jeremiah to take Hanamel's purchase offer at face value and to buy the land. So two copies of the sales agreement are written, probably on papyrus. One of them is sealed; the other is left open. If anyone ever became suspicious that the text of the open copy had been tampered with, it would always be possible to check the open copy against the sealed copy. Jeremiah then instructs Baruch, his trusted secretary, to store both copies in a clay jar (32:13-14).

Jeremiah's Prayer

The account of Jeremiah's purchase of land in Anathoth raises the question of why God would have Jeremiah do such a thing. There are two main reasons to question this move. The first is the most obvious one: Jerusalem is under siege, the fields of Anathoth are under foreign occupation, and Jeremiah is in prison. On a purely secular level—the level of Zedekiah and Hanamel—it makes no sense to buy this field at this particular time. Jeremiah, however, is aware that his action is a prophetic one. His action says that the exile will not have the final say: "Houses, fields and vineyards will again be bought in this land" (32:15). Accordingly, Jeremiah does not struggle with this aspect of the purchase at all. He confesses to the Lord, "Nothing is too hard for you" (32:17).

Jeremiah's prayer nonetheless makes clear that there is a second reason to question this purchase. Jeremiah knows God is the great Creator, and by saying "Nothing is too hard for you" (32:17) he alludes way back to God's covenant promise with Abraham, when Sarah had laughed at the idea of bearing a child in her old age (Gen. 18:10-14). In this way Jeremiah not only acknowledges God's sovereignty but also reminds God of his promises and faithful actions for his people. After a few comments on God's dependability in reacting to his people's attitudes (32:18-19), Jeremiah elaborates on God's power in redeeming his people from Egypt (32:20-22). In short, Jeremiah praises the Lord as the powerful God of creation, the powerful God of the covenant, and the powerful God of the exodus.

To Jeremiah, the siege of Jerusalem and the upcoming exile are understandable. He makes this clear both by means of the structure of his prayer and through some of the vocabulary he uses, such as "sword, famine and plague" (32:24). Israel's disobedience in response to God's grace could only result in disaster (see Lev. 26:23-26; Deut. 28.)

And at this point in his prayer Jeremiah expresses his amazement about the land purchase (32:25). He believes the people have called the curses of the covenant upon themselves. The exile, after all, has been foretold in the law as the necessary outcome of disobedience. *Why, then,* Jeremiah wonders, *would the Lord now revoke the curse of the law?* Jeremiah is puzzled with God's grace because he has a proper, spiritual understanding of history, based on the law of Moses.

The Lord's Response

The Lord's answer affirms Jeremiah's understanding of history at every point, going into even more detail about the Israelites' unfaithfulness than Jeremiah has done (32:30-35). But the Lord prefaces his response by means of the rhetorical question "Is anything too hard for me?" (32:27), challenging Jeremiah to take the words of his own prayer seriously, as noted in the study guide. The remainder of the Lord's answer shows (1) that the power of God's grace is able to overcome even the curse of his own law; and (2) that God will overcome this curse in line with the same covenant document that called for the curse of exile. The Lord reaffirms the symbolism of Jeremiah's purchase of the land, saying that he will bring back his people and have a close relationship with them, that he will renew their hearts and make an "everlasting covenant" with them (32:37-40). The exile will not be the end of God's people Israel.

This assurance of grace is intended to remind Jeremiah that God had already promised a return from exile and a new covenant when he had warned about the curse of exile. The Lord uses some of the same expressions found also in Deuteronomy 30:1-10, where Moses promises restoration after the punishment has taken its course. The Lord thus tells Jeremiah that the curse *cannot* have the last word (32:36). If the coming exile is the necessary outcome of the law of Moses, so is the blessing that follows the curse.

The specific promises (32:42-44), as well as the symbolic action of the purchase of a piece of land, were only partially fulfilled when King Cyrus of Persia allowed the people to return in 538 B.C. In *The New Testament and the People of God* ([Minneapolis: Fortress, 1992], pp. 268-70) N. T. Wright has argued persuasively that in the minds of first-century Jews the exile had still not come to an end. Only with the coming of Christ did the exile truly come to an end, when Jesus took the curse of the law upon himself (Gal. 3:13). In Jesus the "Book of Consolation" has come to fulfillment, the blessings of Deuteronomy have come to pass, and the new covenant has dawned.

Additional Notes

32:9—Jeremiah buys Hanamel's field for 17 shekels (or about 7 oz.) of silver. It is not known how much silver was worth at the time, or how large the property was. Therefore, it remains unclear whether Jeremiah bought the land at a reasonable price.

32:17, 27—The idea that "nothing is too hard for the Lord" occurs again in the angel's words to Mary when the promise of the new covenant goes into fulfillment (Luke 1:37). Jesus also uses the expression to tell us that even the rich can be saved (Matt. 19:26; see also Eph. 3:20; Phil. 4:13).

32:30—The language of this verse is similar to that of Deuteronomy 31:29, where Moses predicted Israel's unfaithfulness to the law and the Lord's subsequent punishment. As the Lord here adopts Moses' vocabulary, he indicates to Jeremiah that the Babylonian invasion is indeed the fulfillment of the curse of the covenant.

32:37-41—There are several parallels between this passage and the law of Moses. Compare Jeremiah 32:37 with Deuteronomy 30:3-5; Jeremiah 32:38 with Exodus 6:7; Jeremiah 32:39 with Deuteronomy 6:2 and 30:6, 8; and Jeremiah 32:41 with Deuteronomy 30:9-10.

32:40—The main difference between the old and new covenants is that the new one will not be broken by people's unfaithfulness. The new covenant will be everlasting (Isa. 55:3; Jer. 31:31-34; Ezek. 16:60; 37:26; Heb. 8:7-13; 10:15-18).

General Discussion

1. *We often hear the expression "Face reality." Think of a recent example in your life in which you may have "faced reality" but did so without acknowledging the intersection between reality and religion. How could you have dealt with this situation differently?*

People often find it difficult to apply Old Testament passages to today's living. This question intends to help us draw a line from this specific historical event in Jeremiah's life and the life of Judah to various situations we might face today. If you like, you could start your discussion by noting the change from the historical context of Jeremiah's day to our day. Jeremiah lived under the old covenant, but we live under the new covenant in Christ, which means that our reality is stamped even more than it was before with the truth of Jeremiah 32:38, in which the Lord declares that we are his people and he is our God.

Group members may struggle with the fact that at times they still "face reality" without acknowledging the underlying dimension of religion in relation with the one true God, despite the arrival of the new covenant. After group members have reflected on and shared about such times in their lives, note together that this discouraging situation offers a number of opportunities for mutual upbuilding:

- We may encourage each other to trust in the power of God's Spirit, since nothing is impossible with God (see Additional Notes on 32:17, 27).
- We may marvel together at God's forgiveness: when Christ came to put an end to the exile, he did this by taking his people's suffering and exile upon himself "even [to] death on a cross" (Phil. 2:8), giving to us the blessings of the covenant and the forgiveness of our sins. In this regard we can also marvel at God's forgiveness despite the way we sometimes "face reality" without remembering how God is in control of reality (see Heb. 10:15-18).
- In addition, we may focus together on the promise of the completion of the new covenant by comparing Jeremiah 32:38 to Revelation 21:3.

2. *Conversely, think of a time when you or someone you know of stepped out in faith, trusting in God's promises. Try to describe this experience in terms of religion intersecting reality.*

This exercise offers an opportunity to switch from looking at our shortcomings to rejoicing and praising God for working in our lives and helping us to grow closer and more aware of our dependence on the Lord. Invite everyone to share an example he or she can think of. As leader, be prepared with an example of your own to help the others get started.

3. *The question "Is anything too hard for God?" (Jer. 32:17, 27) plays an important role in this episode. In what ways might*

this question be misused? Explain. How do we determine when to use it and how to use it in the right way?

The purpose of this question is to caution people not to take the confession of God's omnipotence and run blind with it. For example, career choices based on Philippians 4:13 ("I can do everything through him who gives me strength") but without taking one's given abilities into account can hardly expect the Lord's blessing. Or, in another light, some situations of abuse may take victims a lifetime of struggling to forgive past wrongs and of trying to forge new relationships. While nothing is too hard for God, this does not mean that we should fall for Satan's attempts to make us dare God and put him to the test (Matt. 4:7). As leader, you could point out as well that Jeremiah 32 describes God as bringing about the blessings he promised long before in Deuteronomy. God has not promised to give us perfection in this life; we still live in the tension between the "already" and the "not yet" of God's coming kingdom. With God's Word and Spirit in our hearts and minds we may prayerfully try to gauge when and how to remind ourselves—and perhaps even others—that "nothing is too hard" for God.

4. *How do our prayers compare to that of Jeremiah in chapter 32? Having looked through this chapter, do you see any need for change in your prayer life? Explain.*

Since prayer plays a major role in this chapter, your group discussion may naturally lead into this topic. Note, for example, that the Lord gives a clear, immediate answer to Jeremiah's prayer—an encouraging point, especially as today we may ask our Father for anything in the name of Jesus (John 14:13; 16:24). In his answer to Jeremiah, the Lord points the prophet back to his revelation in Scripture, which already in Deuteronomy has announced the blessings of a new covenant. As we look for answers to our prayers, we do well to remember that the Lord leads us in line with the Word in which he has revealed himself to us.

Although Jeremiah is puzzled, he extensively praises God. He praises God's sovereignty, which the Lord has demonstrated in the deliverance of his people. Regardless of the situation, praise may never disappear from our prayers, especially not as we live in the age of the new covenant, in which God has begun bringing the new-covenant promises to fulfillment. As Jeremiah pours out his concern before God, we are reminded that no questions are too trivial for the Lord. Even our personal worries are important to the Lord, since religion intersects with reality even on a personal level. Nonetheless, Jeremiah's focus is on the people as a whole. In an age that glorifies individualism, we are called, as the church, to be the light of the world. Christ's love should compel us to remember both the church and the whole world in our prayers.

Ideas for Small Groups

Opening (5-10 minutes)

Pray—Ask the sovereign God to guide you in your discussion of this lesson, giving you wisdom by the Holy Spirit to find out what it means to do everything through our Lord, who gives us strength (Phil. 4:13).

Share—Share together how you've been doing on the goals you've set in previous lessons.

Focus—Keep the following question in mind throughout this session: *What does it mean in my life that "nothing is impossible with God" (Luke 1:37)?*

Growing (35-50 minutes)

Read (Optional)

You may wish to read together some sections of Jeremiah 32 (for example, 32:6-9, 16-17, 21-28, 36-44).

Discuss

Before choosing some of the process questions below, work on some of the General Discussion questions (especially questions 1-3).

On God's power and grace in my life:

- Describe any new perspectives that have been opened up to you in this lesson with regard to God's power and grace.
- Reflect on examples of the Spirit's power that you have seen in your congregation lately. Share one or two of those examples with the rest of the group.
- In which areas of your life do you wish God's power and grace would be more evident? In light of this lesson, what should your attitude and approach involve? (See General Discussion question 3.)
- How could your congregation improve in showing God's power and grace to the world?

Goalsetting (5 minutes)

Try to work on the following goal in the coming week:

- Since "nothing is impossible with God," I want to be an instrument of the grace that God's power can work in this world. I want to apply this insight, with the Spirit's guidance, in the following areas:

Closing (5-10 minutes)

Preparing for Prayer

Share some of the things you would like others to bring to the Lord in prayer for you. Mention things that concern you directly, including praise items you want to bring forward. Also remember goals you have set.

Prayer

Address God as the God who has shown grace and blessing to his people Israel, as the sovereign God with whom all things are possible. Invite group members to join in with items mentioned during the preparation for prayer, including items of thanksgiving and praise. Close your prayer by asking the Lord's blessing on what you have learned in this lesson and on the goals you have set. Before parting, you could conclude with some songs of praise, such as "Now Blessed Be the Lord Our God" and "God of All Ages, Whose Almighty Hand."

Group Project (Optional)

Some or all of you may be interested in a cause that looks ahead in hope. When God's kingdom comes in all its fullness, we will live with God, the earth will be restored, wars will cease, and pain and suffering will be no more. Check with health, welfare, political action, denominational, and environmental agencies for ideas and for help in getting started.

For example, you might help in a local immunization clinic, a blood drive, or a food program. Or you could clean up a roadway, waterway, or disaster site. You could also get involved in legal justice and community safety. Or help with literacy and basic-skills education, biblical literacy, acceptance and education of mentally impaired persons, responsible medical research, preservation of wildlife, proper use of land, or purification of air and water. Every area of our lives and of this world is under Christ's authority, and he calls us to seek his kingdom and his righteousness even as we live in this world (Deut. 20:19-20; 22:6-7; Ps. 24:1-2; Matt. 6:33; Luke 12:31; Eph. 1:9-10; Rev. 22:1-2).

13 The Fall of Jerusalem

Jeremiah 39:1-14; 40:1-6

The entire book of Jeremiah has prepared us for this moment: Jerusalem is taken; the palace, the temple, and the people's houses are set on fire; and the walls are broken down. In fulfillment of the prophecy of Jeremiah 1:15, several Babylonian officials take seats in the Middle Gate (39:3). Zedekiah flees in the direction of Jericho, but soon he is captured and taken to Nebuchadnezzar in Riblah, in Syria. There Nebuchadnezzar puts out Zedekiah's eyes after killing the king's sons and nobles. After this humiliating punishment, Zedekiah is exiled to Babylon, where he will die (52:11). All of this happens in fulfillment of the words of the prophets (32:4-5; Ezek. 12:12-13). Only some of the poorest people are left in the land to take care of the vineyards and fields (Jer. 39:10). Judah no longer exists as a nation.

Jeremiah's Emotions

Jeremiah's reaction to the destruction of Jerusalem is not mentioned at this point. But it is clear that this event hurts him deeply. Whenever he has prophesied the downfall of the city and the house of David, he has done so with pain in his heart. How he wishes that the false prosperity preachers had been right (28:6)! Repeatedly his eyes have filled with tears when he has thought of the prospect awaiting Jerusalem (8:21-9:3; 13:17; 14:17). In the book of Lamentations we hear him cry out in grief, "My eyes fail from weeping, I am in torment within, my heart is poured out on the ground because my people are destroyed, because children and infants faint in the streets of the city" (Lam. 2:11; see 3:48). When we see Jeremiah weeping over Jerusalem, we see in him something of the great Prophet who approached Jerusalem on a donkey, weeping over the judgment that was about to burst upon Jerusalem once again (Luke 19:41).

Throughout our study we have seen Jeremiah as a man whose feelings and emotions play an important role. We have empathized with his fear when he is first called to be a prophet (lesson 1). We have felt his despair and his pain in the face of persecution (lessons 5, 7, 9, 11). Continually we have marveled at his courage in the face of his many difficulties. Jeremiah has eaten God's words, which are sweeter than honey but which also bring bitterness and suffering for the sake of God's Name (15:16-18; Ezek. 3:3, 14). The prophet has remained God's servant while suffering at the hands of but also "among his own people" (39:14).

Jeremiah and Nebuzaradan

Nebuchadnezzar has heard about the prophet from Judah. Undoubtedly he is pleased with the rumors he has heard. Imagine a prophet from the rebellious nation of Judah urging his king to surrender to the invading Babylonians! From his headquarters in Riblah, Nebuchadnezzar issues an order to the commander of his imperial guard, Nebuzaradan. He is to give Jeremiah the red-carpet treatment. So Jeremiah is released from the courtyard of the guard (39:14), where he has been confined ever since Ebed-Melech pulled him out of the cistern (38:12-13, 28). Most likely the Babylonians do not immediately release Jeremiah but first take him to a holding camp in Ramah, about five miles north of Jerusalem, on the border between the tribal lands of Ephraim and Benjamin. The misery in the camp is there for all to see, smell, and touch. It's the place where Jeremiah hears Rachel's voice weeping for her children (31:15; see Matt. 2:18). It's the place where Nebuzaradan finds Jeremiah among the prisoners.

Nebuzaradan confirms to Jeremiah the truthfulness of his prophecies. Throughout the years Jeremiah has warned the people of Judah that they would be exiled. Now that the Babylonians are here to exile them, Jeremiah's prophetic message is vindicated. The many prophets of peace and prosperity are proven wrong, and Jeremiah is put in the right. Nebuzaradan acknowledges it: "All this happened because you people sinned against the LORD and did not obey him" (40:3).

Jeremiah Among the People

With these words of vindication still ringing in his ears, Jeremiah is given a choice: he can either take the reward of a good life in Babylon or stay behind with the poor people in Judah (40:4). Jeremiah deliberately chooses the latter. Three times we read that Jeremiah remained "among the people" left behind in Judah (40:5-6; see 39:14). He does not opt for Babylon but for his own people. Jeremiah's insistence that Judah has had to surrender to Babylon has not sprung from a pro-Babylonian stance; rather, it has come from a heart of love for his people, among whom he felt at home and whose annihilation he wanted to prevent. Now that it's too late for the people to repent and most of them are deported to Babylon, Jeremiah knows that he still needs to be a prophet "among the people" who are left behind.

Jeremiah's remaining "among the people" sets him in contrast with Zedekiah. Zedekiah, who refused to surrender to the Babylonians, ends up as a blinded prisoner in Babylon, alone and far away. Jeremiah, who urged the king to surrender, will himself stay behind "among the people." When the Lord comes to his people in judgment, the tables are turned. Zedekiah, the king of Judah, is bound with bronze shackles and taken to Babylon. But Jeremiah, the king's prisoner, is freed and kept from harm (39:12; 40:1). (Ebed-Melech, the Cushite servant, is also rescued—39:17-18.) Nebuzaradan, a Babylonian official, speaks the word of God (40:2-3). And Jeremiah, a reviled prophet, is vindicated "among the people" (40:6). Jesus' words sound as a commentary on these chapters from Jeremiah: "Whoever wants to save his life will lose it, but whoever loses his life for me will save it" (Luke 9:24).

Additional Notes

39:1—The Babylonians laid siege to Jerusalem in January 588 B.C.

39:2—The city wall was probably breached on July 18, 587 B.C. Some sources, using a different method of date calculation, cite the date as 586 B.C..

39:8—As the study guide shows, this chapter's description of Jerusalem's fall and Zedekiah's exile are in fulfillment of God's prophetic word. (Other descriptions are found in 2 Kings 24:18-25:21, 2 Chronicles 36:11-21, and Jeremiah 52.) By saying that the Babylonians "broke down" the walls, this verse looks back to Jeremiah 1:10, where God appoints Jeremiah to "tear down." The same Hebrew verb is used in both passages.

39:11-14—Readers will notice close parallels between 39:11-14 and 40:1-6. And we may wonder, *Do these two passages describe the same event or two subsequent events?* Most likely they describe the same event. We have noticed earlier in our study that Jeremiah sometimes gives somewhat different descriptions of the same event (see 7:1-15 and 26:1-6; 37:11-21 and 38:1-13). If the passages described two separate events, that would mean Jeremiah had been captured again after his release from the courtyard of the guard (39:14) and then transported to Ramah (40:1), where Nebuzaradan then released him a second time. In that scenario it would be difficult to explain why the text makes no mention of a recapture. It would also seem strange that someone of Jeremiah's stature, who was released at the command of one of the highest Babylonian officials, would somehow erroneously get caught up in a transport to Ramah. It seems more likely that Jeremiah was taken from the courtyard (39:14a) and brought to the holding camp in Ramah, where he was then released (39:14b; 40:1, 6).

39:14—Gedaliah is introduced here for the first time. In 40:5 he is mentioned as the new governor over Judah. Gedaliah was a grandson of Shaphan, who had read the newly found Book of the Law to King Josiah in 622 B.C. (2 Kings 22:10). Gedaliah's father, Ahikam, had saved Jeremiah from a sentence of death after his temple sermon (26:24; see lesson 3). We have also met Gedaliah's uncle, Gemariah, and his son, Micaiah, in lesson 6 (36:10-11, 25). Another uncle of Gedaliah, Elasah, is mentioned in 29:3. Clearly this was a leading family from which Jeremiah received a great deal of support.

General Discussion

1. *When the hard facts of life turn out to be truly hard, it may be difficult to see the Lord's name in the story of our lives. How does this lesson encourage us nevertheless to look for God's presence in our lives?*

The study guide contrasts Nebuzaradan and Zedekiah. Nebuzaradan's comments to Jeremiah indicate that the Lord's name is present in the story of Jerusalem's fall, even though Zedekiah refuses to acknowledge that fact. The Lord wants us to live our lives in the awareness that the name of Jesus has been proclaimed over our lives.

Recognize together, though, that it is not always possible for us to see the Lord's hand in events. To confess the Lord's hand in important historical events is one thing, but to claim that we can trace that hand in concrete political and military happenings is another. The same is true in our personal lives. To confess the Lord's involvement in our lives is one thing, but it is often impossible to say why certain things happen in our lives. Be careful not to underestimate the struggle of people who have to endure great difficulties and who have nagging questions about the Lord's involvement in their lives. Acknowledging the presence of God remains a matter of faith, and it remains something that people will struggle with in faith.

2. *What is so shocking in the contrast between Nebuzaradan's acknowledgment of God and Zedekiah's shallow understanding of life? How does this story present a message for us today?*

This question draws attention to a feature that also came up in lesson 11, where we noticed a contrast between Zedekiah and Ebed-Melech. The element of contrast plays a role throughout the book of Jeremiah: Jeremiah stood over against Pashhur (lesson 5), Josiah over against Jehoiakim (lesson 6), the prophet over against the people (lesson 7), the exiles over against the survivors (lesson 8), Jeremiah over against Hananiah (lesson 9), and the messianic king over against Zedekiah (lesson 10). In these conflicts and contrasts the Lord vindicates his servants, and ultimately Jesus Christ is vindicated as the "righteous branch" (23:5).

The contrast between Nebuzaradan and Zedekiah is particularly disturbing because Zedekiah, being a Davidic king, should have known that Judah's unfaithfulness was leading to its destruction. As the leader of his people, Zedekiah was positioned to acknowledge the Lord's name and thus prevent the impending disaster. The irony here is that as soon as Zedekiah has failed in his task and the destruction of Jerusalem is a fact, we hear a Babylonian commander explaining the reason for the disaster. This presents a warning example to Christians today; we should proclaim the name of Jesus and his lordship in our surroundings. You may want to focus together on how you as individuals, group members, and church members can proclaim Jesus' name and lordship in your everyday activities. Be specific in your examples.

3. *Rather than going to Babylon, Jeremiah stayed behind "among the people" (40:6). In what way does this action remind us of Jesus Christ? In what way(s) can this action encourage us?*

The true humannness of Jesus is no less important than his divinity. Jesus shared in our humanity so that he could destroy the power of the devil (Heb. 2:14; 1 John 3:8). In fact, not only did Jesus have to be human; he had to be a Jew, a son of Abraham (Heb. 2:16). Jesus had to really be "among the people" of Israel. As their representative King, he could identify with his people and thus draw their punishment upon himself. The punishment that Zedekiah and his people had to go through—the exile—was something that could be undone only by a true son of Abraham (a Jew) and a true son a David (a king), who would stand in the midst of his people and take their place.

This means there's hope for all who look to Jesus for their identity in order to belong to God's people. There's encouragement for all who present themselves as subjects of the Son of David and want to follow their King. Christians have a Savior and Lord who is really one of them. As one of them, he is able to sympathize with them (Heb. 2:18; 4:15). Seeing that Jeremiah stayed "among the people," Christians can be assured of the faithfulness of Jesus, who took his place "among the people" for their sake.

4. *This final lesson in our study may seem to end on a negative note: the fall of Jerusalem. Explain why we can argue that even at this dark time the positive side of the picture is more pronounced than the negative side.*

The destruction of Jerusalem is indeed a horrible sight. Jeremiah's book of Lamentations makes that point clear. The history of God's people has come to a horrible end because of the people's consistent unfaithfulness, which has characterized the story of Israel ever since it began in the days of Abraham (see Gen. 12:10-13). This lesson presents the end that was to be expected ever since Moses presented the law in Deuteronomy.

But the fact that this moment has been anticipated also means that the Lord is behind it. Nebuzaradan rightly states, "The LORD your God decreed this disaster" (Jer. 40:2). One positive element in this climactic story is that it does not present unconnected, random events; the Lord is clearly at work in them.

We may also know that the fall of Jerusalem does not have the last word. The law of Moses, as well as the prophets (including Jeremiah), has stated that there will be a turnaround after the exile. The people will come back. The Lord will forgive their sins. He will set up a new, everlasting covenant with them. As we noted in lesson 12, the exile is the dark gateway to a future in which the light of the Lord's message—God's good news—will shine more gloriously than ever before. Today we know that this message shines by the light of Jesus Christ, the very Son and Word of God.

Ideas for Small Groups

Opening (5-10 minutes)

Pray—Thank God for the opportunity to reflect on his Word together. Ask the Lord to use this chapter about the fall of Jerusalem to rebuild you as a group and as a part of God's universal church.

Share—Share about progress you have made, as well as difficulties you may have encountered, in working on goals you have set during this study. Which ones will you continue to pursue?

Focus—Keep the following question in mind throughout this session: *What does it mean to me that the Lord's name (Jesus Christ) has been proclaimed over my life?*

Growing (35-50 minutes)

Read (Optional)

You may wish to read the Scriptures for this lesson before moving into your discussion time. Or you could read just 39:4-7 and 40:1-6 to focus on the contrast between Zedekiah and Nebuzaradan.

Discuss

General Discussion questions 1 and 2 deal with the heart of this lesson. After doing some of the General Discussion questions, look at some of the process questions below.

On the presence of Jesus' name in my life:

- Cite one or two ways in which this lesson has helped you see that the name of the Lord Jesus is proclaimed over your life.
- How could you use the Scriptures for this lesson to encourage somebody who has a hard time seeing the Lord's presence in his or her life?
- Mention one or two ways in which your congregation could show more awareness of Jesus' lordship over all areas of life. (*Leader:* Draw the group's attention to the Group Project in lesson 12.)

Goalsetting (5 minutes)

Try to work on the following goal as a result of this Bible study:

- Since the Lord has proclaimed his name over every aspect of my life, I want to acknowledge his lordship in the following ways:

Closing (5-10 minutes)

Preparing for Prayer

Mention a few things you would like the other group members to bring to the Lord for you in prayer.

Prayer

As you come to the end of your study of the life of Jeremiah, praise the Lord for using people like this prophet, who was willing to eat God's words and suffer the consequences. Praise God especially for bringing the exile to an end in King Jesus, and ask the Lord for eyes of faith to see the power of his name in your lives. Remember together also the various prayer requests that group members have brought forward. Pray that God will fill each one of you richly with his Spirit so that the lordship of Christ may more and more take hold in your lives. Ask for courage and wisdom to follow Jesus faithfully in all kinds of situations—good or bad. Close your meeting, if you like, with a doxology, such as "Now Blessed Be the Lord Our God" or "To God Be the Glory."

Evaluations

Before your group members leave, please ask everyone to fill out the evaluation form at the back of the study guide. Your answers and suggestions will help us as we develop other studies in the *Revelation Series.* Thank you! Please mail your evaluations to

Revelation Series / The Life of Jeremiah
CRC Publications
2850 Kalamazoo Ave. SE
Grand Rapids, MI 49560